# Managing with Asperger Syndrome

*of related interest*

Asperger Syndrome Employment Workbook
An Employment Workbook for Adults with Asperger Syndrome
*Roger N. Meyer*
*Foreword by Tony Attwood*
ISBN 1 85302 796 0

How to Find Work that Works for People with Asperger Syndrome
The Ultimate Guide for Getting People with Asperger Syndrome
into the Workplace (and Keeping Them There!)
*Gail Hawkins*
ISBN 1 84310 151 3

Employment for Individuals with Asperger Syndrome
or Non-Verbal Learning Disability
Stories and Strategies
*Yvona Fast and others*
ISBN 1 84310 766 X

Succeeding in College with Asperger Syndrome
A Student Guide
*John Harpur, Maria Lawlor and Michael Fitzgerald*
ISBN 1 84310 201 3

Asperger's Syndrome
A Guide for Parents and Professionals
*Tony Attwood*
*Foreword by Lorna Wing*
ISBN 1 85302 577 1

Build Your Own Life
A Self-Help Guide for Individuals with Asperger Syndrome
*Wendy Lawson*
*Foreword by Dr Dinah Murray*
ISBN 1 84310 114 9

# Managing with Asperger Syndrome

*Malcolm Johnson*

Jessica Kingsley Publishers
London and Philadelphia

First published in 2005
by Jessica Kingsley Publishers
116 Pentonville Road
London N1 9JB, UK
and
400 Market Street, Suite 400
Philadelphia, PA 19106, USA

*www.jkp.com*

Copyright © Malcolm Johnson 2005

**Library of Congress Cataloging in Publication Data**

Johnson, Malcolm, 1967-
Managing with asperger syndrome / Malcolm Johnson.-- 1st American pbk. ed.
p. cm.
Includes bibliographical references and index.
ISBN 1-84310-199-8 (pbk.)
1. Johnson, Malcolm, 1967---Mental health. 2. Asperger's syndrome--Patients--Biography. 3. Asperger's syndrome--Patients--Employment. 4. Asperger's syndrome--Patients--Life skills guides. 5. Executives--Mental health. 6. Psychology, Industrial. I. Title.
RC553.A88J64 2004 2005
616.85'88--dc22

2004010972

**British Library Cataloguing in Publication Data**
A CIP catalogue record for this book is available from the British Library

ISBN 1 84310 199 8

Printed and Bound in Great Britain by
Athenaeum Press, Gateshead, Tyne and Wear

# Contents

# Preface

I decided to write this book in an attempt to partially fill a gap in understanding that I perceived existed in the outside world for those professionals with Asperger Syndrome (AS): that is, to provide an insight into the effects and impact of AS on those who work in management or white-collar positions.

Much has been written about high-level autism and its impact on those affected by it. There are also, it seems, numerous books about employing those with autism at the lower end of the scale offering advice on the difficulties that they are likely to face, how they can adapt to the workplace and how they can improve their performance and situation.

However, there is much less information about people with mild forms of Asperger Syndrome who may be employed in middle-management positions, with all the attendant responsibilities. Since discovering that I almost certainly have Asperger Syndrome, I have found very little written material that has provided any background, guidance or direction that can assist me in coping with the pressures and demands of the professional workplace, or in overcoming some of the difficulties that the condition places upon me.

I have not tried to write, nor do I claim that this book is, an authoritative guide on Asperger Syndrome. Instead, it seeks to convey my experiences in a working environment in a number of middle-management positions and the difficulties that I have encountered. It also describes some of the lessons that I have learnt and the actions that I believe can, and have, mitigated the effect of these difficulties.

What perhaps struck me most when writing this book was that the problems that I encountered, and the solutions I have advocated to reduce their impact, were, in the main, much the same as those that the average person also has to face and implement. Perhaps they are magnified and exacerbated somewhat, but the same problems they appear to be.

The end result is that I feel I have gained confidence: not that I could completely remove the difficulties that I have experienced, but I recognise that I was, to a large degree, perhaps in a not entirely dissimilar position to those around me. This has helped to reduce my feeling of 'differentness' and made me feel that I can fit in more easily. The more I learn and understand the easier it becomes to do so.

Much more needs to be learnt, and the experiences analysed, of those with Asperger Syndrome. Very little is currently available. I hope, however, that the following text will provide some insights that the reader can recognise and build upon and act as a catalyst for additional reflection as well as identifying further ameliorative actions.

It is important for the reader to note that I became aware of my condition shortly prior to my joining the BBC, a period that is covered in the penultimate chapter of this book, 'Productivity and Efficiency'. Many of my experiences, and therefore lessons, were derived before this occurrence and it would be appreciated if this could be borne in mind as the book is read.

# Asperger Syndrome: What is it?

Asperger Syndrome is a mild and high functioning form of autism. Named after the Austrian paediatrician Hans Asperger, the condition remained largely ignored from its discovery shortly after the Second World War until the early 1980s, when it began to receive greater prominence.

Recently, as more has become known about AS, there has been an increase in the level of publicity about the subject. A significant reason for this is that it is believed that many of those affected by Asperger Syndrome have special savant skills or even a spark of genius about them. Among those thought to have been affected by the condition are Albert Einstein, Isaac Newton and Bill Gates.

It is believed that AS predominantly affects young males. Hans Asperger in his original diagnosis was drawn to particular traits among the boys he studied: those of being insular and abrupt. Over time, he came to recognise that this was not due to their being obstreperous; more pertinently, it was the result of, among other things, a poorer ability to socialise and relate to others to the same degree as other people.

There are a number of symptoms associated with the condition which may or may not be apparent, or are only so to varying degrees. Perhaps the most common aspects are exceptional levels of independence and insularity and more limited social skills. People with AS are regarded as being 'in their own world' with a lack of desire, need or ability to relate fully to others. They do not seek social contact and have poorer social skills in general which means that they are less well equipped to easily form and maintain relationships. From a personal perspective they are conscious of feeling 'different' to other people and this sometimes makes them apprehensive when in company, especially groups.

Those affected by AS are also thought to lack the ability to fully 'mind read': to effectively discern the thoughts and feelings of others, so failing to respond to or meet other people's emotional needs. As a result, they are often regarded as aloof, difficult and cold individuals.

The inability to 'mind read' is also reflected in an inability to recognise facial expressions. People with AS themselves sometimes have 'wooden' faces that fail to respond to the non-verbal signals of others. In particular, there is a lack of eye contact (which indicates, erroneously, a lack of interest or failure to pay attention) when interacting and a failure to use gestures to augment verbal delivery. The latter itself may be monotonous and lacking in any variance in tone. Motor skills may also be poor.

Those with AS tend to have highly rigid modes of thinking and interpret things in a literal fashion. Though they are capable of very original ways of thinking, they often fail to think laterally or to consider alternative viewpoints. However, it is their originality in thinking that is thought to be behind the unique and advanced abilities of certain people.

Being in their own world means people with Asperger Syndrome are often unaware of, and uninterested in, the nuances of social protocol. They dress practically, as opposed to fashionably, and are often uninterested in the everyday things that appeal to their contemporaries. This only emphasises further their individuality and 'differentness' leaving them further exposed and vulnerable to the influences of the social jungle.

An inability to mix can often lead to particular difficulties when forced to socialise. This is especially so in groups. In one-to-one situations, a person may communicate fluently, feel at ease and be able to hold a quite normal interaction. In a group setting, however, the pressure of being among a number of people and the need to harmonise and contribute can induce apprehension and anxiety, causing the person with AS to withdraw.

Attention Deficit Disorder (ADD) may also be apparent. Here there is difficulty in concentrating for periods at a time, particularly when the subject matter is outside an area of personal interest. When the subject is of special interest, however, the effect may be quite different. Here a person may be able to remember seemingly endless information in great detail. It is not uncommon for a person with AS to have an almost photographic memory about specialised subjects, such as periods of history or car number plates, in which they have a particular and close interest. As a result, such people find it difficult to absorb and remember some data or concepts quickly. Often the minds of people with AS will wander onto a subject matter totally unconnected with the material currently under discussion and the person will appear to 'switch off' to the activity around them.

Opinions vary as to the cause of AS. One possible explanation is a mild form of brain damage as result of a rapid birth as was the case with me. This damage may affect certain areas of the brain associated with memory and information processing. Because of this, cognitive skills are less developed in some areas than usual, though often only to a small degree, making learning slower and more problematic. This makes the task of identifying people with AS more difficult.

Finally, people with AS like routine. Change is something that they find stressful and seek – often unconsciously – to avoid. They follow rigid patterns of behaviour, often for long periods of time, and are comfortable with the status quo.

The above are not the only factors that relate to Asperger Syndrome, but one thing is beyond question: people with AS are different and, as a result, they develop rich, and very different, inner worlds.

# 1 Introduction

'Yes: but what about the consumer?'

I was in a meeting with the new divisional director – a former marketing professional himself – whose first words to me were this question. Starting with the consumer is, after all, what all professional marketers are taught to do, for building a product that meets the needs of consumers is the central objective of marketing! It was therefore an obvious question for anybody who worked in marketing to ask a fellow professional...but I just could not think straight or find the correct answers.

It was easy enough when I thought about it later, when I wasn't under pressure; all the subject matter and related detail came hard and fast: core audience 15 to 24 – in other words, teenagers and young adults; totally product-led; and a price barrier of around £5.

Having said that, this was no ordinary meeting. It was the first time that we had met the new divisional, main board director. He was a hard, aggressive, 'give-the-answers-to-me-straight' type of character whose approach represented a change in the management style that I had been accustomed to, and change is something that, as a person with AS, I was uncomfortable with.

The meeting had been sprung on us with deliberately at short notice so that we had no prior warning or indication what to expect. We had been told at four o'clock on the previous Friday afternoon to report to the head office at nine o'clock on Monday morning, and the managing director, who had met the new director a couple of times before and knew what he was like, had not mentioned anything. I was totally unprepared.

What was worse was that I knew why he was asking these questions, but felt unable to provide the correct answers. The business approach of the company was essentially financial in emphasis and totally contrary to the central objective of marketing – namely, investing in products, services and promotion to satisfy the needs of customers.

Consequently, the shortcomings and negative image that I believed surrounded the company's core product were not being addressed even though I believed – and had argued passionately – that they should have been. The company hadn't provided me with the resources: indeed, the senior management did not understand why it was necessary. Every time that I had advocated doing research to identify consumer needs so that marketing activity could address the identified shortcomings, I had been met with a negative response. If I had spoken the truth in this meeting with the new divisional director, it would have meant putting my boss in a poor light: but being anything other than totally truthful and loyal as dictated by my Asperger Syndrome was something that I found uncomfortable and virtually impossible to do!

As the questions came hard and fast I felt under even more pressure. The room was packed with colleagues and I was aware of them watching. It was the sort of tense group gathering that I had never handled well. I began to feel not just nervous but frightened too: I was conscious of being in deep trouble.

In order to focus more fully on the actual questions, and cognitively process the information more effectively, I turned away so that looking directly at the director didn't distract my thought processes. But he didn't like that; the loss of eye contact, as typically practised by those with Asperger Syndrome, made him even more suspicious: 'I should warn you, young man, I have a nasty habit of checking these things.'

It was all very different at my initial interview with the company four years earlier. I didn't know what to expect then either when I went in to meet the person who was to become my future boss; he could have been an ogre as well, but he wasn't.

'Good morning, Sir!'

'George, please call me George.'

Only he and I were in the room and as I was required to interrelate with only one person at a time, a person who immediately put me at ease,

I did not feel anxious. His welcome was totally reassuring and so was his questioning: always constructive, always positive; and I sensed, and felt, that it was entirely honest too – I was completely comfortable being able to say what I thought, irrespective of whether it was positive or negative. But, there again, George was an exceptionally bright, straight and highly respected person who had the knack of supporting, encouraging and motivating people.

As the questions came, so naturally did my answers. I felt able to respond positively and say honestly when I did not know what the answer was: I liked that. I left thinking that this was a place I would like to work and a person that I wanted to work for – a person that I could trust and be loyal to, and learn a lot from: just the sort of person who would bring out the many positive, beneficial characteristics inherent within Asperger Syndrome. The whole process felt 'right' and I knew that I had got the job.

With hindsight, knowing now about my AS, I can easily explain my reactions in the previously described crunch meeting. However, at the time I had no idea of my condition. I knew that I had always felt different, but I could not explain why. If I had known what was wrong I could have seen the meeting coming, considered things beforehand and prepared for some of the possible potentialities, but I did not. At that stage I had never even heard of Asperger Syndrome.

# 2 What's Been Driving My Bus

My reactions and behaviour in the meeting with the new divisional director, and the way that I have managed people and situations throughout my career, are illustrative of a number of core traits that have been consistently present within my personality from an early stage. Consequently, they have impacted greatly on my management style and performance.

It is said that the major thought processes and actions that guide behaviour throughout life are generated and learnt in the first few years. Behavioural patterns form and continue to appear in different guises at different times, in different circumstances, in different situations and with different people.

These processes may be particularly pronounced for those with Asperger Syndrome as the traits that are associated with the condition are more exacerbated. Looking back, I believe they have strongly influenced me personally and, in particular, my experiences and performance in the workplace.

From as early as I can remember I have always felt different to those around me. I could not explain how or why, but I felt different. Though I did not realise it at the time, this feeling (of being different) has had a major effect on the development of my career and on the way I have interrelated with people and the way they have perceived me.

The source of this behaviour, I believe, lies in important traits that I picked up from my parents: traits which have played a significant part in formulating my actions and that have been highly influential on my interpersonal relationships. These, in turn, have had a further effect on my work-related experience.

My father was, for the most part, an insular, independent man with – often – firm opinions about others. He also possessed what my mother described as a very 'genuine' (in other words, honest) personality, a trait that is pronounced in those with Asperger Syndrome. He had spent his early working life employed by large organisations but was ill at ease in structured, formal working environments. Consequently, he started to work on his own as a self-employed electrician, where he enjoyed a reputation as a likeable, reliable tradesman who enjoyed a high degree of trust.

My father taught me *his* perception of the way that things ought to be done and the way people should behave. He modelled a tendency to express feelings overtly if people digressed from his idea of 'acceptable' behaviour; such a deviation made it hard for him to deal with and relate to these people.

However, this facet, which was impressed upon me, brought many benefits for me. I became, and came to be regarded as, honest, reliable and trustworthy and in possession of a high degree of integrity, all of which have proved to be highly valuable assets throughout my working life. However, perhaps I did not learn to take into consideration all the circumstances or the views of others, or understand the need to exercise tact when forming judgements. As with my father, my views were firm, clear and very black and white and I was often told that I held 'strong views' – something that used to surprise me.

Overall, from my father I developed a very strong sense of right and wrong which is consistent with a major trait of those with Asperger Syndrome: that of being 'honest to a fault' (Attwood 1998). Although this may be an honourable trait, it is one that I have found is not always reciprocated in the corporate 'jungle', which has presented me with certain difficulties. My not feeling able to say what I truly believed in the aforementioned meeting with the divisional director through fear of putting my boss in a critically exposed position is one example. Working to attain a position and stance that I believe in and can defend whenever necessary has become a key personal managerial objective and requirement for me.

The genuineness inherent within my father was also apparent on my mother's side, though often expressed emotionally with fewer inhibitions. Things could upset her considerably and could grate for lengthy periods. From her I gained a tendency to worry unduly about things and to feel uncertain in some situations and with certain people. Like her, if something transgressed the high values and principles I had inherited, I would respond strongly, resulting in a counterproductive response from others and the problem remaining an issue for a considerable period after. I have come to appreciate that it is important to not react emotionally and prematurely to issues within corporate environments and that standing back and retaining distance can deliver real advantages, such as the maintaining of credibility and gravitas.

During my childhood and adolescence I remained emotionally distant from others and this also reinforced my feeling of individuality and 'differentness'. In her book *Thinking In Pictures*, Temple Grandin explains how she has difficulty understanding people whose actions are governed by emotions as hers are guided by intellect. This is something with which I can closely concur as I have a logical mode of thinking.

In addition, I also had little interest in, or appreciation of, many of the interests of other children. I enjoyed cricket and other sports – particularly team games – but did not easily mix or undertake role-play in groups, meaning that I was not the greatest team player. As for TV soaps – I could not see what people saw in them!

I seemed distant from many of the everyday matters that others of my age were interested in and picked up on naturally. Fashion was something about which I was unaware and unconcerned. I never wore things that were fashionable or that stood out. Instead, I wore basic clothes that were practical and comfortable, as opposed to contemporary and trend conscious.

Another important factor during my early years was my (perceived) intellectual ability. From an early stage I was both totally uninterested and non-gifted in practical matters and focused instead on the written word. I was encouraged by my parents academically and came to believe that I was intelligent and intellectually capable.

My early schooling was non-taxing and much of what I can recollect of infant and junior school was basic and, for the most part, consisted of what might now be termed 'child-centred' learning. Though I can remember learning my times tables and basic punctuation such as full stops, if I was taught grammar in any meaningful way I am unable to recall it.

About this time I became aware of streaming and an exam called the 'Eleven Plus'. I was conscious of it being very important and of the need to pass it to get into grammar school. One day, upon entering the classroom after a play break, we found the desks re-arranged and formal papers on them along with pencils. We were told to sit down and complete the paper within a specified time period.

I struggled. The questions were of a type that I had not encountered before and seemed to consist of quite complicated maths, English and puzzle-type tasks. By the time I had finished I knew that I had not done well and was shocked when the teacher informed us that we had sat the first half of our 'Eleven Plus' exam. I was surprised: why had we not been told?

Later in the week, the teacher went back through the paper and explained clearly how to approach the questions. It all seemed much clearer then and by the time the second half of the exam came around I thought that I had done quite well, though not well enough to pass overall.

It was the first more realistic indication of my capabilities; though I was certainly intellectually capable, I was not perhaps as innately gifted intellectually as I had thought or had been led to believe. It seemed to take me a little longer to grasp the underlying principles behind subjects, particularly if I could not relate it to something. For example, at secondary school, though I undoubtedly worked and tried hard, I was unable, as my physics teacher rightly pointed out, to understand fully the fundamental concept that all objects consisted of molecules that were dynamic.

This, however, was the key to my learning: once I had grasped the fundamental point I was able, in most cases, to acquire the necessary understanding to perform well. Working to achieve this is something that I have put into practice successfully in many areas since. Though this was not always possible with subjects such as physics that I struggled to relate to, I did leave school with nine O-levels and three A-levels as a result of commitment and hard work; and four years later, I fully realised my academic capabilities via achievement of a good degree. Now, whenever I am faced with a problem I make my key objective the understanding of the core issue initially, before attending to specifics.

Looking back, however, another issue with certain subjects such as science and maths was that, deep down and in true AS form, I simply wasn't sufficiently interested. What interested me specifically were real life events, people and the world. I could relate to them and place them in an understandable context. In addition, subjects such as history and geography enabled me to utilise what I was quickly coming to appreciate was a real skill – my analytical ability. I seemed to have an uncanny ability to analyse and appraise different real-time life scenarios – opinions about events, for example.

After university, my thoughts turned to what I would do with my working life. As I had progressed through my teenage years I had developed no real interest in the arts or science. Instead, like most in my family, I became fascinated – almost obsessed – with the news and current affairs. It was not uncommon for us to watch the news three times a day. A visit to the Deutsche Presse-Agentur in Germany convinced me that, more than anything in my life, for a career I would like to be a foreign news correspondent for Reuters! However, positions were scarce, meaning that, realistically, alternatives would have to be considered.

My early years, therefore, provided insight into some traits that would impact enormously upon my working career. Recognising these and making sure that I mitigated their negative aspects whilst fully exploiting the undoubted positives that they also conferred, could bring me real benefits. This was to play a vital role in my progression and future achievements within managerial capacities.

# Key personality traits

## A sense of being and appearing different
I was conscious of being different in certain ways to those around me. My behaviour differed from the majority in small but discernible ways, whether it was my introversion or my lack of interest in many of the normal, everyday things in which my peers showed a close interest. Though I would not appreciate this, others would become conscious of it, and reducing this effect in future years has proved important in enabling me to assimilate more closely with contemporaries.

## Independence and insularity
I was largely independent in outlook and practice. I neither sought nor effected great contact with the majority of people and in fact – with hindsight – sought distance. Empathy was not something about which I was conspicuously conscious or to which I attached any great importance. Empathising with others, however, is something I have come to appreciate to be vital – and achievable – and a major contributor to success within the commercial world.

## Integrity
I felt, and generally displayed, a high degree of integrity. Being honest was important to me, and something that I expected of others. I was conscious of being acutely aware of right and wrong. Retaining these traits whilst respecting differing ones in others has made an important contribution towards my developing interpersonal and managerial capabilities.

## Rigid thought patterns
My mode of thinking was very regimented, precise and clear cut. I was quick to formulate opinions and generally unwilling to compromise them. My views were very black and white. However, taking the positives from the often unique insights generated by people with AS and adding them to the input of others has offered me the opportunity to augment my thinking and realise significantly enhanced outcomes as a result.

## Anxiety levels
Things would bother me and I worried. If something became an 'issue' it would become a cause of great anxiety and would remain so for a

considerable period of time. As I have progressed throughout my career, however, I have learnt how to temper this facet and channel my energies more positively so as to relax and work more consistently and effectively.

### Level of intellect and motivation

My level of intelligence was not as innately high as I, and some others, perceived it to be, which, together with my rigid learning mode and tendency to direct my motivation mainly towards those things that particularly interested me, resulted in limited progress in my early years outside of these areas of interest. However, by working to understand the underlying principles of a subject or problem and thereby activating my motivation, I have, I believe, been able to realise achievements significantly above others of a higher intellectual capability.

These factors continued to operate and return in the future and did so to powerful effect in a number of situations in a work environment.

# 3 Initial Work Experiences

My first job after college was in a local hospital working as a handyman doing simple repairs. I really enjoyed it. It was laid back, informal and I wore casual (that is, working) clothes. I worked with two elderly men and I enjoyed that too. They were both avuncular and blue-collar workers; I did not feel in any way intellectually exposed and was not required to fit in with peers. The fact that it did not put me in a taxing (that is, strange) or demanding environment meant that I did not feel uncertain or uncomfortable.

Looking back now I can see that this simple basic job and its working environment provided many of the facets that would suit my working style and requirements which I could identify and look for in other roles in the future. It was:

- informal

- made up of work colleagues from a similar social background with whom I could easily relate

- in an environment and involving a job task that was not intellectually over demanding.

The job was not taxing me, nor obviously, could it challenge me to achieve my full potential; nor was it a long-term option, so I began to search for a career job. After a search process I was offered two 'real' jobs simultaneously. The first was with a large IT organisation that I got via a university 'Milk Round'. However, I could not take up the position until the following October at the start of the next academic year.

Simultaneously, I was offered a position with a US investment bank in the City. Prior to the interview I had not heard of them but after the offer had been received, I became aware that it was a very prestigious organisation with the reputation of having an aggressive operating culture. As the offer from the computer company was open until the autumn, I took up the offer at the bank with a view to trying it for six months until having to make a final decision.

The environment in the investment bank was strange and unlike anything that I had experienced before. First, for the first time in my working life I was required to dress formally every day. Though I did not exactly hate it, I cannot say that I enjoyed it either. I felt ill at ease and uncomfortable in formal clothing and felt unable to feel myself or completely relax. The mode of dress impressed upon me – perhaps subconsciously – the formality, unnaturalness and strangeness of the environment I felt that I was in.

I was also conscious of whether my choice of style, though not unacceptable, was of the type or quality that others adhered to. Being someone who was neither especially interested in fashion, nor in possession of a dress sense beyond that which was practical, I felt unsure as to whether my dress code was appropriate for my surroundings. This, in turn, increased my sense of feeling, and maybe of being regarded as, different.

The pace in the bank was hectic! I supported the traders by preparing simple accounts to track their positions. I especially enjoyed going onto the trading floor where the atmosphere was electric and talking to the traders, many of whom were streetwise, down-to-earth characters. In the main I got on well with them as I resonated with people who I perceived came from my type and level of social background. This significantly reduced any sense of anxiety in my interpersonal relationships and dealings.

The work was relatively straightforward but I felt uncomfortable in other ways. First, I was conscious – as with my dress sense – of being in a formal environment that I did not naturally fit in with. I was also unsure about the material that I was working with. I struggled somewhat to pick up the meaning behind the figures and to fully grasp the concept of accounts. I also felt uneasy about formulating figures which were both high and important in so far as the trader relied on them when calculating his deals: one error could have significant consequences to his position and, therefore, his profitability. As I did not completely understand the workings or mechanics of the City, or finance either, my work matter remained impersonal to a degree meaning that my interest did not fully develop and, with it, my motivation.

As a consequence I became concerned with my future prospects. I could not see where I was going. I was earning pretty good money for somebody of my age and experience but did not believe that the work provided me with any purpose. I felt that I wanted and needed some kind of formal career path and direction. Above all, I wanted to develop a tangible skill for the future and so, six months later, I took up the offer of the formal graduate training programme with the computer company.

I found the switch difficult. The decision to change positions highlighted an important factor and one about which I came to understand a great deal more subsequently. The change was marked and somewhat unsettling. Learning how to deal and cope with necessary change was a skill that I needed to acquire as change is inevitable in the modern business world. Successfully achieving this in the future would result in considerable advantages going forward.

## Dealing and coping with change

In their book *A Guide to Successful Employment for Individuals with Autism*, Marcia Datlow Smith, Ronald G. Belcher and Patrica D. Juhrs argue that people with AS have particular difficulty handling change.

Changes in routine and schedule are disrupting and troublesome to those with AS. They tend to try to – consciously and unconsciously – avoid change by attempting to maintain sameness in the environment, and by performing tasks in the same or a similar way.

Other factors can also have an impact. Change from a supportive to a non-supportive manager can be challenging, and an individual with AS needs to be sensitive to the attitude of new management and attempt to change/influence it through education, good rapport and adequate support.

The authors argue that, if an environment is found that is suitable, then job switching should be avoided. A tolerant manager, tolerant co-workers, informal systems of support and positive reinforcement may all be present and are critically needed. These supports can take time to develop and are not easily replicated. Temptations relating to higher salaries, more interesting work and so on, should typically be resisted in favour of keeping a job that has proven to be stable, tolerant and secure.

Key factors that may assist in coping with change are:

- being open, amenable and less resistant to change

- finding environments that remain broadly the same and jobs that are relatively stable in terms of tasks, routines and scheduling.

Once a job has been learnt it becomes easier to handle change and additional tasks that suddenly appear.

There is, I believe, much good sense in this advice. I have always found change unsettling and tend to feel happiest when I am set into a routine and know what is expected of me by being in a familiar situation and with people with whom I feel comfortable. Until this happens, I remain and feel slightly withdrawn and unable to fully express myself.

My new position resulted in my spending two years in IT. With hindsight, it offered me the opportunity to acquire a high degree of computer literacy and with it skills that I could have utilised throughout my working life and that would have made me relatively independent from an employment perspective.

Though I was unaware of it at the time, IT is one of the key employment areas that psychologists have identified as being ideal for those with Asperger Syndrome, as the logical skills required to work with computers are highly apparent in those with AS. Moreover, as the work predominantly involves interacting with a machine rather than people, it is not an area that demands advanced social skills or the need to form relationships with large numbers of different people.

However, most of the training was largely technical and involved learning about basic programming, operating systems and other related areas and I was unable to relate the material or process to any actual situations. Though I could work out tasks mechanically to a basic level, I found it hard to progress further as I was unable to comprehend satisfactorily the underlying logic or how it could be applied.

A few years later I picked up the programming manual that I had kept and started to flick through it. Being relaxed and under no pressure, it all seemed much clearer; indeed I understood the logic behind it all and found it relatively easy. Not *having* to learn it seemed to make all the difference to my mental approach. I have also come to appreciate that understanding the underlying principle of an issue can vastly improve my work-related learning.

## Really understand what you are working on

For someone with AS, an appreciation and understanding of what one is really working on is, I believe, imperative. By achieving this I have greatly enhanced my work skills and subsequent performance.

A useful way I have found to improve in this area is to actually 'experience' the subject matter, as opposed to just conceptualising it via reading or discussion. During my training I failed to truly understand the rationale behind databases and their management. However, by using cricket statistics as material – an area of strong personal interest – I found that data could be organised and manipulated within a computer database in a relevant fashion.

By putting issues into a practical, applicable and wider context, relating it to material that I am interested in and enjoy, I find that I am able not only to gain an underlying feel for them but also to code the information effectively and thus retain it in the long run. Far from just remembering the information in the short to medium term, I find that I retain it permanently – and clearly! In addition, illustrating my thoughts and concepts in visual form has also greatly aided my thought processes.

The old adage of 'Tell me something and I will forget it; show me something and I will remember; let me do something and I will learn' is, for me, highly applicable!

In time, I was moved away from programming and into a business unit. The area that I was seconded into was financial services as it was felt that my City background would be useful. It certainly seemed to interest me. I found for some reason that I had started to miss the environment of the City's Square Mile. I had started to hear about the effects of 'Big Bang', the deregulation that had been instigated by the government to bring the workings of the financial industry into the modern age.

As a result, I started to read books about the City and developed an interest in the workings of the financial markets. The more I read the more I understood why gilts were sold by the Bank of England, why corporations issued convertibles as well as straight bonds and why the money was raised and the financial instruments were structured in the way they were. Understanding the rationale and the processes behind the work provided meaning and, with it, stimulation and motivation. In whatever job or role I now find myself, I make learning about the business in a deeper fashion a priority objective.

The interest that I began to develop in business as a subject, and the need to know more about it in general, meant that I decided to increase my understanding of it further by going back to university – to business school – to do an MBA.

## Key development points

- Look for work environments that reflect, as far as possible, your personal background and outlook so as to increase the likelihood of your feeling that you 'fit in', which reduces feelings of anxiety.

- Consider your dress sense and seek to find a balance between what you feel comfortable in and what reflects and fits in with work colleagues and the working environment.

- Work to develop a structure and clarity of direction with regard to your work tasks to achieve a greater sense of security within a role. Strive to achieve personal motivation via clear, understandable and challenging objectives.

- Anticipate, understand and learn to accept and live with change. View change as positive and something that can enhance work performance and career prospects.

- Consider and gauge carefully the intellectual requirements of a role. Look for and secure positions that provide a challenging but not excessive level of intellectual demands initially. Avoid positions with excessive intellectual requirements in order to mitigate against stress and realise maximum learning and performance potential.

- Strive to acquire as much knowledge as possible of the chosen area of work, its operations and related issues to aid understanding, motivation and job performance. Identify the meaning behind the job task fully so as to reduce uncertainty and increase motivation via the realisation of specific, individual goals.

# 4 Fitting In and Adopting the Right Approach

I had found out about the MBA qualification from the father of a best friend at school. He was an elderly man, highly intelligent and had left Poland, having fought in the Polish resistance, to come to Britain. He then became an economist for a major insurance company where he commented on political situations from investment perspectives. His advice: learn Russian and get an MBA and you will be made for life!

Well, the Russian was more difficult but getting on an MBA course was less so and in late 1988 I embarked upon one. I immediately felt at home and regained a strong sense of purpose – the subject of business fascinated me.

The course gave me a better overall appreciation of what business was all about and how companies operated. I was especially interested in marketing, most particularly strategic marketing. I enjoyed analysing different scenarios, marketplaces and companies. I seemed to have an excellent intuition as to the dynamics and the key factors that were driving and influencing a business. To me this was the most important thing: correctly gauge the way that a market was going, make the right strategic decision and the rewards were immeasurable compared to just exercising sound financial discipline or being operationally efficient!

I was particularly influenced by the marketing lecturer, which was not surprising as he was highly charismatic and eminent in his field. His special area of interest was retail. His premise was that the retailer in the UK held exceptional power and that working within the retail sector was therefore an advantageous place to be. As a consequence, my objective of returning to the City receded and I decided that I was going to work within marketing for a retailer when I finished my studies.

The other point that is relevant with regard to my business school studies is the theory that I had ingrained in me. I was taught that there were two types of company. Finance-led companies set financial targets and worked towards achieving them. Often these were short-term goals that were achieved at the expense of long-term viability. Most British companies, it was argued, were finance-led organisations. Another category was those that were market-led: in other words, those that identified consumer needs and sought to build market share over the long term by satisfying them. To achieve this, organisations needed to forego short-term profitability to ensure long-term prosperity via the investment that was required to build market share and achieve the profitability that was a function of it. It was a powerful message and one in which I believed strongly, and would subsequently have confirmed to me by experience. Perhaps, also, it was the only view that I really seriously considered.

I enjoyed my time at business school. It was interesting, motivating and beneficial and I believe that it gave me a sense of direction for my career. However, I also developed, as perhaps did many MBAs at that time, a slightly false sense that this piece of paper was everything. If you had an MBA, it was believed in some quarters, you were fully equipped to run a business and assume a senior role. It was perceived by some as some kind of super qualification that bestowed upon its holder high-flying status. Whilst this may have been true in some cases, in reality the situation for me and many others was that it was a first-class qualification that was an excellent tool providing a framework upon which I could build in the future.

With hindsight, however, I had not fully understood or absorbed parts of the subject matter. As is the case for someone with Asperger Syndrome, areas that had interested me I had worked hard at and taken in; areas that did not were only superficially imbedded. Finance, in particular, had been inadequately understood and appreciated!

Upon graduation I began to look for a job. The first position post-business school would be a particularly important one. It was where I would apply the theory and concepts I had learnt and build on the framework that I had been given. In addition, it was the time when I would be gaining an initial foothold on the senior management ladder.

Where someone works post-MBA is also important from a cultural perspective and even more so for a person with AS. There are some companies that are very pro-MBAs, seek to recruit them, know how to integrate and utilise them and how to get the best out of them. There are other companies who do not and whose working environment is not geared towards applying the theory and the concepts that an MBA confers.

Looking back from a personal, AS perspective, what I really needed post-graduation was to work not only within the former type of organisation but also within an environment that was professional and stable. I also needed one that would have enabled me to build on the foundation that I had laid and on the enthusiasm that the course had engendered. I needed to work with professional staff in a professional environment, one that was secure and that would have enabled me to settle in and acquire the technical, day-to-day marketing skills that the MBA did not provide.

More importantly, I also needed to acquire practical, everyday experience – dealing with people, using interpersonal skills, encountering real situations that called for skills such as tact, common sense and ground-level awareness, so that I could add to the excellent strategic skills that the course had provided. I also needed, from an AS perspective, an environment that was supportive. In short, I needed a professional, undemanding setting where I could have grown steadily into the role. As it happens, I unintentionally ended up in a company and a role that did not provide these benefits.

The interest in retail that I had developed at business school meant that upon my graduation I approached retailers for a position. Retailing today is a highly sophisticated, well-developed and dynamic sector.

At root level, however, retailing is a seat-of-the-pants, intuitive and rough-and-tumble type of marketplace. Though many of the companies that I had approached were modern, professional operators, the firm into which I was accepted still had, to a large extent, an old school approach and mentality.

I had an initial interview with a personnel manager and then met the marketing director. He was a big, larger-than-life character. He talked about getting fresh blood into middle management. Though the status of the role was outlined, the exact nature of my tasks, duties and objectives were not. But that did not matter; I was going to work in retail, in marketing, and that was the most important thing! After a third interview which, given the marketing director's approval of me beforehand, was a formality, I was offered a job.

I had done some initial research about the company prior to my interviews and learnt a bit about it. Though a major player which had grown rapidly by acquisition, the company had recently undergone a management buyout that had resulted in the current management assuming power.

It had been a contentious and hotly contested takeover during which the ethics of the new chief executive had been brought into serious question by his behaviour, as he had initially colluded behind the former management's back and then changed allegiance. The end result was a corporate culture and an atmosphere that had been highly affected by the takeover process and the management style of the characters of the winning team. Not for the first time, I was to experience the influence that the man at the top was going to have not only on the company but also on all those working below.

## Analyse your choice of environment

The working environment that a person with Asperger Syndrome needs is, in my opinion, the most important factor when considering a vocation and position. When assessing any potential position there are issues that I carefully examine about a potential employer and role.

First, as a person with AS, I have found working in high-pressured, unstable, rapidly changing work environments unsettling. I find that I need time to learn and grow into a role and until I get on top of the job task, I tend to experience anxiety when subjected to extreme pressure. This, and changes in the workplace and my routine, can also have an unsettling effect.

As a result I prefer, and look to work within, supportive corporate environments, as opposed to aggressive ones, as the atmosphere and work ethos generated by such cultures will exacerbate the negative aspects of Asperger Syndrome. Moreover, poor political, social and communication skills are likely to mean that an AS affected manager will find it more difficult to deal with those events and issues that are likely to arise more readily from within such cultures.

I therefore ask myself when considering any job offer: What type of a marketplace does the company operate in and what type of company is it? What is its culture? What is the history of the organisation and the industry within which it operates.

I look for companies that exude stability to generate a supportive and progressively constructive corporate culture geared towards delivering long-term business success. In general, I look to avoid aggressive, politically charged environments, where there is rapid change and where employee development is not a high priority. The culture in an aggressive organisation is unlikely to suit the honesty and high values of a person with AS. Moreover, constant change will result in uncertainty and anxiety.

Second, I ask: What is my role and where does it fit within the organisation's structure? What are my key objectives, what do my specific duties involve/encompass and what are the implications of these for my AS? What am I expected to achieve, in what timescales and with what resources? I seek to define clearly what the company's expectations are of me. What skills does the role require and how closely do these match mine? Can I exploit fully my particular talents? Are there any skills that are strongly required that I do not possess? Importantly, does the role necessitate building relationships with a wide variety of constantly changing, different people? Is there a lot of hard bargaining required?

Importantly, I question whether the role and tasks are likely to involve/necessitate dealing with high levels of organisational politics and the forming of sensitive relationships. Does the role put me into areas of high pressure and conflict? If so, I seriously question whether I am equipped to deal with the situation.

Third, and very importantly, I look at whom I report to and what their personality is. What is their character and style of management? To whom do they report and where do they sit in the wider scheme of things? I look for changes and possible disruption higher up.

The later chapters of this book will highlight the difficulties that I have had with working alongside, and for, certain types of manager. My experience has shown that it is essential to have the support of your immediate superior whoever you are. For a person with AS it is even more critical. I seriously evaluate and gauge the extent to which I can work for someone.

Do they share the same outlook and similar values to me? Are they the type of manager who seeks to engage in meaningful debate and conversation? Above all, are they likely to be personally supportive of me?

In summary, I look for an environment, an organisation, a manager and work colleagues with whom I can fit in and develop a relationship over the longer term. These factors are not universal, nor are they easy to find, but they are well worth searching for and, for a person with AS, critical.

In many ways, these recommendations are no more than what any ordinary job hunter should do when researching a job. The important thing I remember is that I am not an ordinary job hunter and, consequently, I need to explore the above aspects even more carefully than the average person needs to if I am to avoid ending up in the wrong situation. Importantly, I think deeply about each facet and what its implications are for me.

I commenced work with my immediate boss who was atypical of the company. He was highly educated, courteous and capable, but he was also, perhaps, unsuited to the culture of the company, having come from a retailer widely regarded as one of the more professional and respected on the high street into an operator which, in many ways, was the complete opposite.

My initial role was to conduct analysis of the catchment areas for new stores around individual towns. The market leader had focused its revival strategy on developing a state-of-the-art location-finding function, as access to a store was vital to the consumer and therefore critical to the success of the company.

Whilst the market leader had devoted significant resources to building their highly skilled, location strategy team, I was to work with a colleague under the director and build a unit from scratch. To assist us was a small space planning team that analysed sales data and made recommendations for store layout and product composition. I was warned that the man who headed it up was 'not easy to work or deal with' and that I needed to be careful when approaching him for the information I required.

I developed a good relationship with my boss. Easy-going, erudite and seeing in me a kindred spirit, he was someone with whom I worked well. In addition, I seemed to be getting on well with the space planning manager and not encountering any hostility or obstruction.

Over time however, the same could not be said of my relationship with many of my other colleagues. I had been forewarned prior to joining the company that there was some opposition to my joining at a high level. I was seen as a high flyer and regarded with suspicion.

With hindsight I did not help myself by reciting views and theory from business school that, in many ways, were like 'a red rag to a bull'. It agitated people and provided fuel for criticism that could be used against me. It was not that what I said was necessarily wrong: it was the way I was saying it!

How anyone acts and behaves in a corporate context is important, but it is another potential obstacle for a person with Asperger Syndrome. I have found that if something is of particular importance to me I will promulgate it strongly. By emphasising my qualification (MBA), I was inadvertently exposing myself to criticism.

## Act in a way that is appropriate to your surroundings

I have learnt that being sensitive to, and adapting to, different environments, though not easy for me, is imperative. An important practical requirement that my experience has impressed upon me is the need to assimilate and fit in with the demands of the working environment – both physical and personal.

Whilst at the investment bank I was conscious that my style of clothing, though smart and perfectly acceptable and presentable, was out of sync with that of many of my contemporaries. The need to 'fit in' in this way was something that I never considered important or appreciated very deeply due to my individualism and the lack of importance that I attached to the subject.

However, style of dress is important, I believe, for credibility. As a senior manager I have found that it sends a message; more pertinently, for someone with AS, failing to adapt sends an additional signal: you are different and your failure to fit in acts as a partial reinforcement of differentness and eccentricity.

I make it an objective to try and limit my insularity by keeping my 'personal uniqueness' to a minimum. It is not being different per se that is the issue; but it is important to be sensitive to others around you so as not to impact negatively upon them. Whilst remaining myself, I try to accommodate the views and styles of the environment and those I work with and respect both them and the culture that presides within the organisation.

I soon became aware that I was failing to build sufficient rapport personally with my work colleagues. At the beginning my subordinate was friendly and respectful towards me, even inviting me to his house for a social occasion.

Over time, though, this changed. His demeanour became frosty and he resented having to draw information from his PC that only he could access because of the unique (to the department) PC skills that he possessed. I put this change of attitude down to the fact that, as my boss put it, 'John's a strange lad.'

My other peers, who had been cautious of me to begin with, then started to become more distant towards me. One, whose personality was brash, became openly critical. I could not understand why.

The perception of me being withdrawn that people began to form was also to re-appear later during my career at the BBC. As a senior manager I had an office to myself, something that I liked as it provided solitude and meant that I was able to work independently without being concerned about those around me.

Even though my staff sat just outside the office I would usually communicate with them via e-mail. It was easy enough. Short messages could be sent more easily this way than by getting up and walking outside simply to ask one of them something.

However, it sent out a negative message. Later, one of my staff, when I enquired after my management style, stated that they would prefer that I approached them personally. I had not thought it important, but they did; the message that it was sending to them was one of distance and they interpreted it as my being indifferent to them. Despite mixing fairly openly – or so I thought – the impression that I was conveying was otherwise.

## Mix and build rapport

The insular and introverted personality of a person with Asperger Syndrome inevitably means that mixing and building relationships with others is unnatural, sometimes difficult, a low priority and possible source of anxiety.

I have found that even if I do not have to work directly with people all the time it is both essential and beneficial to secure consensus and support. As a senior manager I have come to appreciate greatly the value of being approachable and on the same wavelength as others to gain their support.

As a person with AS I have often found it difficult to mix and naturally prefer my own company. Consequently, I have tended to avoid socialising and attached little importance to it personally.

However, it *has* to be done, and made a high priority, in order to function effectively as a senior manager. People will view a person with AS suspiciously if their insularity and slightly eccentric lifestyle are pronounced. By withdrawing, these facets are compounded; by mixing and socialising, people understand better and feel more at ease with the person. So, at every opportunity I do socialise – and not just with the few people with whom I work closely or get on particularly well, but with as many colleagues as possible. I have found that reaching out and widening contact with people brings innumerable benefits in a variety of areas.

After an initial few months, the company decided to appraise its strategy. The strategic direction of the company was unclear and had been of concern to senior management given the changes that were taking place in the market overall. Consequently, it was decided to bring in outside consultants to undertake a strategic review.

I was delegated to become part of a small, dedicated, high-profile team that was put together to conduct a top-level, strategic appraisal of the business. The project was very high-profile within the company and a great deal of store was placed upon it. In the words of the Chief Executive: 'This is probably the most important project yet undertaken in the business.'

Unbeknown to me at the time (due to my ignorance of my condition), the project was to place me in a problematic situation. First, I had not been with the company long and had insufficient knowledge of its culture, current business strategy or the marketplace in which it operated. Consequently, my technical knowledge was limited and likely to be a shortcoming.

Second, my relationships with my colleagues were not yet fully developed and some of their caution towards me meant that they were less likely to be sympathetic towards me if the going got tough. I would, therefore, be hindered in terms of support.

Third, the project was highly politicised. The outside consultants not only had a reputation to protect but also needed to be seen to 'deliver'. There was always the possibility that this would produce tensions.

The consultancy had a reputation of being high-powered. Its corporate culture was highly distinctive and viewed critically by fellow companies within the consulting sector. Fitting in with its style of working was never going to be easy. In addition, their lack of in-depth understanding of the marketplace, or the industry that we operated in, meant that they would rely on standard consulting tools and analysis to derive their conclusions and recommendations. This was never likely to fit easily with a down-to-earth, street operator-type retailer.

My first task was to collate information relating to competitors and their strategies – work that I enjoyed and excelled at. However, from the beginning a fellow colleague more senior and experienced than me, one who viewed the project as an opportunity to raise his own profile, started to question the work that I was doing. He did not agree with it, think it was accurate or what we should be putting forward.

I failed to stand my ground adequately. Rather than argue my case, I prevaricated and demurred. The uncertainty that I felt increased, and with it the consultants' uncertainty towards me. I began to doubt myself and felt like a square peg in a round hole within the formalised consultancy style of working.

The project was regarded by senior management within the company as a failure. The consultants were thought to have not addressed the real issues and were providing masses of information and proposals that were regarded as being of little practical relevance. Overall, the consultancy did not come out of it well: nor did I personally as a result. The whole environment had proved totally unsuitable for me and I left the retailer after a year. The experience had impressed upon me the need to find the right kind of corporate environment within which I could work. I had, though, learnt some important lessons, ones that I could, and would need to, take on board during my career.

## Key development points

- Identify the right working environment by analysing an organisation and its operations carefully. It is important that there is a good 'fit' between the work environment and your personal outlook, and that there are relevant support systems.

- Evaluate the existing organisational culture: Is it supportive and collegiate? Is it constructive, focused on long-term objectives and likely to support the values of someone with AS? Will it provide an opportunity for you to feel able to contribute?

- Question carefully what is required of you personally. What does your role entail and what are your key objectives? Do your skills match the set objectives and can you deliver? Are the tasks and responsibilities ones that you are prepared for and capable of doing?

- To whom will you report? What is the character and management style of this person? Consider carefully whether this is someone with whom you can work closely.

- Tailor your approach to your surroundings and work environment. Be sensitive and receptive to the culture that pervades within the organisation and among work colleagues; try to assimilate to this culture.

- Seek to limit your 'differentness'. Dress and act appropriately and keep personal mannerisms such as self-verbalisation under control.

- Be open to, and proactively mix and engage with, colleagues to build rapport. Be open to everyone and not just your immediate circle, and ensure that you are approachable.

- Ensure your personal views, opinions and preferences are guarded and voiced in measured terms, sensitively and tactfully. Appreciate and acknowledge the views of others.

# 5 The Right Environment: an Ideal Position

My next job was as a marketing executive of a subsidiary of a major leisure organisation. The company's policy was to advertise internally and I acquired details of the role via a contact before the role was advertised externally.

It immediately caught my eye. There seemed plenty to it: promotions, PR, new store openings, managing the internal marketing award scheme. There was a bit of everything, just what I needed and the right type of role to get me started properly in marketing. The job seemed unpretentious and clear in its requirements and I secured an interview. I waited outside the director's office until I was asked to enter.

'Good morning, Sir.'

'George, please call me George!'

Whereas the project with the internal consultants whilst working at the retailer was, with hindsight, always likely to be difficult for me, the interview with George was a ready made, perfect setting for me to be myself and to shine.

First, the interview was on a one-to-one basis. There was no group pressure, no need to reconcile different characters, views and approaches, only the requirement to communicate with and impress the man in front of me.

The surroundings, too, were unpretentious. Though I did not realise it at the time, this was an important factor in the way I felt. The office was old and, though decorated and tidy, was without any of the trappings that one would normally expect to find in the office of a chief executive. There were certainly no illusions of grandeur: indeed, it was comparable to the type of surroundings that I had come from and was used to – basically very down-to-earth.

Most importantly, I immediately sensed the type of person I was dealing with: entirely straight, honest and wanting to have a constructive, positive conversation. There were no games or trick questions, no personality tests and the only thing he seemed to be interested in doing was finding out who I really was and what I was about.

I felt relaxed and at home from the first moment. I had not actually prepared very well for the interview, though, in a perverse way that helped to relax me – because I was not desperate for the job I came across as composed and confident. I was able to answer most questions intelligently and perceptively because of my business school background, and never at any time did I feel that the job that I was being interviewed for was beyond my capabilities.

I do remember what may have been an important moment: I was asked a question to which I did not know the answer. I looked out of the window and pondered for a moment before turning to George and replying, 'Sorry, I don't know.' 'That's all right,' came the immediate, reassuring reply.

All of the time I was conscious of the fact that, though I was being sized up, I was able to speak frankly. For example, I explained that I had very little promotional experience and that I did not believe that I was the finished article, but that with George's support I could do the job and grow further into it.

Before the end of the interview George asked me if I wanted the position and I said I did. 'I can't say that you have actually have got it,' he said, 'but put it this way: you can say that you are 90 per cent of the way there. I just need to think about one or two things a little further.' That he was prepared to say so was a clear reason for my thinking that I had been successful and that was a major boost to my confidence. I left on a real high and with a feeling that I wanted to be there and, above all, to work for this person.

I was called back for a second interview ten days later and this time I prepared more thoroughly. But this time I was simply asked about my enthusiasm for the position which I reiterated. I was offered the job a couple of days later and entered a position that was to be the most fulfilling and enjoyable of my working life.

At a later stage I asked George why he had chosen me and one of the reasons he gave was that he saw a person who would fit in and one who would grow into the job. The former point was very evident from the moment I walked through the door and felt comfortable and at home. This is the factor that I feel that a person with AS needs to locate most in a working environment so as to be able to flourish and achieve their (undoubted) full potential!

## The ideal boss

At the time of my interview with George I did not know about my Asperger Syndrome. However, in any position, especially for a person with AS, getting on with your superior is essential. Without the support of the person above you no senior manager can operate effectively. From my experience, I think I can safely say that if you lose the confidence and support of the person above you, even marginally, your ability to deliver is impaired: if you lose it in any meaningful way, the effect is likely be terminal!

For a person with Asperger Syndrome these points all hold true but doubly so; but there are others that are also vitally important.

### Support and assurance

As a person with AS I find that I need support and reassurance to work effectively and efficiently. I need to know that the work that I am doing is acceptable and satisfactory; I find that I am motivated by acknowledgements and recognition of accomplishments.

### Motivation

The support and approval of your boss is essential to provide motivation. As is often the case for someone with AS, I sometimes find motivation difficult. It is not because I do not want to do something, but more simply finding the urge to do things at times is lacking. Praise and encouragement I have found are the best motivators for me.

**Mentoring**
The right kind of boss will act as a mentor providing assistance with adapting to the culture of the workplace, integration, learning the job task, and so on. As a later (also excellent) boss was to say to me, 'A bad boss teaches you bad habits and you should never work for one'.

George provided, and was, all of the above…and more:

- Support: At all times I believed that I had George's support and that acted as a constant assurance. This gave me the confidence and security that I needed to relax, grow into the job and develop further – which I did.

- Motivation: Praise and encouragement were certainly in abundance. If something was done well you were told so without hesitation. If something was lacking it was pointed out constructively and always couched in positive terms. One of the things that I find most debilitating is negative criticism or the 'run-someone-down' approach/delivery. This was never apparent with George. All observations were positively couched and this helped to spur my motivation and greatly enhanced my work commitment and performance. Even when I was being praised there was usually an additional constructive, intelligent comment to finish with that enabled me to learn further. At the close of a meeting, after a particularly busy and demanding week, I would always leave the office ready for more challenges!

- Mentor: His knowledge about everything was seemingly enormous. I always learnt something. Advice was practical and intelligent and whilst I felt that I was being guided I was also being challenged personally, which aided my development.

- Protector: George seemed to enjoy a joust. It was almost like a game to him. He got on with everyone and dealt comfortably

with contentious issues. If things ever did get heavy there was
the feeling that he would be there to deal with it.

- Open and approachable: George was totally honest and
  candid. He was open. I felt that I could discuss anything with
  him and that no games were being played. Every Friday, I
  would have a one-to-one meeting at which we would go
  through everything that I had done, and been involved with,
  that week. One thing that I find extremely unsettling and a
  cause of anxiety is being unable to reassure my superiors of
  what I am doing. Partly this is due to the need to be reassured
  that what I am doing is correct and what is required of me,
  but also I need to feel that my superiors know what I am
  doing. Each week, therefore, I had the opportunity to meet
  and do this and I felt much happier as a result. I always try to
  ensure that there is a line of regular communication open to
  my superior to enable me to do this.

- Integrity and honesty: A person with AS is likely to feel
  uncomfortable at best with anyone who is less than honest.
  Personally, I find it virtually impossible. If the vibes that I am
  receiving are less than certain or suspect in this area, I am ill
  at ease. I need to have open, frank and honest dialogue. If I
  have it, I find that I can openly express myself and prosper; if
  not, I cannot. George was entirely trustworthy and this was
  another valuable source of reassurance that enabled me to
  settle well into the role.

I was going to take over from Roger who was taking early retirement after
a considerable period of service. Roger was a gentleman: courteous, polite
and ever willing to help.

The offices in which I was going to work were old, antiquated and
had a touch of the past about them. The department was a small,
close-knit one and my work colleagues were down-to-earth and similar
in outlook to me. Most had been with the company for a long time. I felt
an affinity with them and was immediately relaxed and comfortable.

I had my own room in the corner of the office, which afforded me
some privacy. It was somewhere that I was not under the constant
watchful gaze of others, but that enabled me to meet my fellow workers

naturally throughout the course of a day, when I needed to. It was quiet, so I could concentrate, and it had a good aspect.

I had a couple of staff working under me, which was the first time that I had really had to manage people. Neil was younger than me by about four years. A graduate, he was slightly rebellious in the nicest possible way and keen on promotional work – I would rely on him significantly in that area as it was not something of which I had any experience or knowledge. My secretary Helen was a temp who had worked for Roger for a short while. He spoke highly of her. She was diligent and seemed to be a conscientious person.

The company was a subsidiary of a much larger organisation and, at the time, one of the UK's largest companies. It had a rich heritage and stature, along with a reputation of being slightly staid and stuck in the past. However, it was stable and not cutthroat in culture and the general feeling that exuded was one of trying to build on and retain something that was both worthwhile and which people valued. George was right: it comprised both the sort of environment that I would fit into and the type of people that I would get along with.

The market in which the company operated was also exciting, which made it a fun place to work. I began to not only feel at home but to really enjoy it. I was content within the small department, and what was happening throughout the rest of the company was of minor importance as far as I was concerned. Moreover, George was there to support me. My confidence was high and I felt as though I had landed on my feet, such was the degree of comfort that I felt within the environment and with my colleagues.

## The right corporate environment

From a vocational perspective, the major factor that needs to be sought by a person with Asperger Syndrome, particularly at senior management level, is the right environment in which to work.

What is 'right', though, depends on individual and personal circumstances. The environment within the leisure company was certainly 'right' for me!

### Corporate culture

The corporate culture within the company was stable, supportive and collegiate. It was not cutthroat or ruthless and I felt at ease with its style and objectives and not pressurised in any way. I also empathised with the objective that I interpreted as working constructively towards a worthwhile outcome.

### Similar work colleagues

I was working alongside people who came from a similar background and shared similar personal characteristics. This is something that I now look keenly for, as it makes assimilation and the forming of relationships easier for me.

What type of people these are depends on an individual's personality and personal attributes. In the leisure organisation these were supportive, good-natured people and so were not contrary to the outlook of someone with AS. Intellectually I found they were not excessively above my level, meaning that I felt comfortable and was able to communicate easily with them. They were down-to-earth, informal, unpretentious people with integrity.

### The physical layout

The fact that I had my own office that enjoyed a reasonable degree of privacy meant that I was not exposed to, and was therefore less conscious of, those around me. Having my own space benefited my concentration and my work productivity. To work optimally, I need to keep disruptions to a minimum, be it in the form of personal intrusions, distractions such as noise or other surrounding events. If my space is personalised I find it helpful. Overall, the atmosphere was informal and I find that the more this is so, the better.

Overall, the leisure company provided all these facets meaning that it was an environment that enabled me to feel comfortable, express myself and fit in.

## Key development points

- Identify and search for the type of senior manager with whom you can work: specifically, one who displays high levels of integrity, openness and trust and who provides support and, in the early stages, can act as a guiding mentor.

- Ensure that channels of communication are open with an immediate superior to encourage regular dialogue and the means whereby understanding and approval of work can be gained to provide a means of motivation.

- Maintain close contact with, and have the support of, your immediate superior to ensure that a safety valve from high pressure is maintained.

- Acquire a personalised workspace that affords a degree of solitude and provides you with the opportunity to work quietly and independently to reduce personal exposure.

- Look for a company that exudes a positive, constructive and supportive working environment, one with which you can empathise and whose values and objectives match your own as closely as possible, with personnel and management that share these characteristics.

# 6 Understand the Politics

The organisation that I had joined was not market-led. Though well-established, its market share had been slipping for a number of years as new competitors had entered the marketplace and built new, more attractive and functionally more efficient developments.

The root problem was that the parent company, by imposing highly demanding investment criteria, had failed to invest sufficiently to maintain its position. Though the parent company was earning impressive profits, the market shares enjoyed by each of the subsidiaries, including our company, had been falling for some time. In addition, there was virtually no marketing (as I understood it to be) going on within the company.

One of my first tasks was to meet my fellow executives outside of my immediate, small department. Most were well-established: 25 years' service was nothing and many had done far more. There were two executives about five years older than me making me, at thirty, the youngest by far.

The various executives performed a variety of functions: administration, development and retail sales, and there were five field or operations executives who were responsible for the units in the field and who seemed to enjoy a fair degree of influence. They all had different characters, including Bill who seemed innocuous and unassuming. All were immediately likeable and resonant of the constructive atmosphere that pervaded the company.

One of the executives did, however, make a comment that was to assume importance later: 'Historically your department has never been held in very high esteem within the company or by the managers'. This observation did not make any undue impression on me at first. As a person with AS I was mainly conscious of my immediate surroundings and colleagues, and what was going on elsewhere in the company was, to a large degree, irrelevant and unimportant.

As part of my induction I worked my way around each of the regions and spent a day with each of the field executives. Upon my return, I chanced into a conversation with a colleague who asked me my views about each of the field executives. I truthfully explained that I liked them all. When asked specifically about one of them – Bill – I was able to reiterate that he had been fine with me; I was, however, warned to be cautious, as he could be very temperamental.

After a short period of time it became clear that Bill was a significant figure within the company. At executive conferences he was always seated next to the managing director for the evening dinner. This was not his choice. I was told that the accepted word on the executive grapevine was that Bill would succeed George when he retired in two years. He was highly thought of and had the vital, specialised experience of having worked under George for a few years previously.

The importance and relevance of this information did not register with me. In my career to this point I had never been exposed to corporate politics in any meaningful way and was therefore unaware of its significance.

Though I had studied organisational behaviour as part of my MBA, I had given little thought to the politics that existed within the company, nor was I especially likely to, given my lack of exposure to it at that point.

Consequently, I was virtually oblivious to it and naively unconcerned about its potential effects. I simply attached no real importance to it at all; as far as I was concerned, I could concentrate on what I was doing and not become involved. As a result, I made no conscious attempt to ascertain how the land lay in this area or to make a judgement about it.

## Being aware of and
## understanding office politics

Every manager needs to be aware of, and deal with, corporate politics, as it exists in every organisation and is an unavoidable facet of corporate life. Basically it revolves around personalities and the building of interpersonal relationships. Because of my condition it was an area that I was not naturally disposed to engage in. However, I subsequently have found it to be one of the most important and also most difficult areas that I have to deal with.

As with dealing with AS itself, I have found the first requirement is to become more aware of what the politics consists of and what are its possible consequences – both positive and negative. In her excellent book *Office Politics: A Survival Guide* Jane Clarke defines politics as 'derived from the Greek word "polis" which means city state – the organisational structure introduced to help create some order in a society with many diverse and, sometimes, conflicting interests' (Clarke 1999, p.4).

All companies, according to Clarke, are political: it is just that some are more so than others. However, politics does not automatically mean negativisms. Office politics implies the acquisition and utilisation of power to achieve what you want. Clarke asserts that this practice can be constructive or destructive. It can be driven by the selfless concern for the general corporate good or by purely selfish motives. An individual needs to decide which it is in each instance and then make a judgement.

Clarke describes effective office politicians as those who know where the power lies, who understand how to obtain it for themselves and who possess the skill to use it to pursue their own goals. This is constructive when the individual is concerned about the organisation's success, but destructive when the motivation is selfish or unethical or if unacceptable methods are deployed to achieve those ends. The last point immediately rings warning bells for me; a person with AS is acutely sensitive to what they believe is right and wrong or ethical.

According to Clarke, those managers who view it as important to understand office politics tend to have a positive view about what it could do for the organisation; those who do not, consider it to be destructive and unhelpful. By natural inclination, I typically fell into the latter category. I found it hard to understand why anyone would want to engage in political infighting as I viewed it as negative and destructive. For me, the most important things are trying to get on with people, and doing a good job.

As the atmosphere within the leisure company in general was friendly and collegiate, there were very few warning signs of danger in this area.

Issues such as change, excessive competition, complex structures and personal advancement are all political causes of friction, and potentially sources of problems and acute difficulty for a person with AS. As a result I have found the need to continually ask:

- What type of politics is operating here?

- What is its/the person's motives?

- What are its potential consequences for me?

I try to view the position objectively and positively and not assume that it will not affect me or that I will not be exposed to its negative side. One aspect of my condition is that I have sometimes in the past rather naively believed that if I naturally retain my distance and do not engage in political activity, I can remain immune from both it and its consequences.

In my experience as a senior manager, getting on up the corporate ladder and surviving in an organisation depends to a large degree on being an effective politician. This applies whether you have AS or not, but if you have, it is doubly important. I have found that I am likely to be even more susceptible to effects and consequences of office politics due to my difficulty in effectively gauging, understanding and dealing with it.

Today, as far as possible, I try to steer clear of any politics. If I can avoid highly politicised companies I do so, and I try not to get into highly politicised situations – such as the consultants' strategy overview in the retailer – in the first place. As a manager and, in particular, as one who has aspirations of going higher, however, I inevitably come across politics and therefore have had to learn how to deal with it, or at least mitigate against its effects in relation to my condition!

Experience has taught me that I need to learn to live with organisational politics and to make understanding it one of my highest managerial priorities. The key to this, I have found, is to understand and appreciate where power lies.

# Power in organisations

There has been much written about the subject of power in organisations. It can be formal or informal power and the latter, in particular, I have discovered can be found in unlikely places and among people at relatively low levels within the corporate hierarchy.

Jane Clarke provides an uncomplicated overview of power in organisations that I have found particularly useful and which provides an invaluable framework for ongoing evaluation. It centres around four types of individual, all of whom I can identify with, who are of importance and provide a basis for initial analysis.

### Opinion Formers

These are also known as Important Others. They exert an important degree of influence over what happens irrespective of their position. These people are important and there is a need to form effective relationships with them. You need to understand the way they are thinking and earn their respect.

### Gatekeepers

These people seem to control the information flow around the company. They open and close channels of communication and regulate the speed with which information is released. They also filter details in such a way as to effect the message that they wish to convey.

### Repositories

These people have a wealth of information and knowledge often built up over a time via experience or by being aware of what is going on around them. They should be consulted and used to assist your decision-making process.

### Cliques

These are informal groupings that inevitably develop in any organisation. They may come together because of a common interest – either officially or unofficially. Again, their effect can be positive or negative and one needs to be aware of them.

All of these figures with hindsight became recognisable to me within the leisure organisation.

Most important of all is the Opinion Former. Though I did not appreciate it at the time, Bill was an Opinion Former or Important Other. At executive conferences critical assessment and decision-making seemed to gravitate to, and rest to a large degree on, Bill's viewpoint. His opinion was always sought and largely followed.

I have come to appreciate that identifying the Opinion Formers is vital and achieve this by watching closely for those whose views are consistently sought and taken on board. I make special attempts to build relationships and form links with these people by making the effort to proactively engage with them.

There were also two key Gatekeepers within the organisation, one towards whom one could be positively disposed and one requiring a more guarded approach. The former was the financial director who accrued huge amounts of information from various sources to centralise the financial position of the company and whom I quickly came to trust. Possessing a high degree of integrity, the financial director issued information that was always accurate and reliable.

I also became quite quickly aware that the managing director's secretary was an important source of data, but being in a position of confidentiality meant that she could only divulge information that was more limited and sometimes incomplete. Furthermore, information was also actively sourced from this outlet and I came to appreciate the need to be careful when seeking and proffering information. Overall, I came to understand that Gatekeepers were largely those through which important, day-to-day information would pass.

I found that Repositories were generally numerous and scattered throughout the company. Often these were people who had been in the organisation for a long period of time and were lower down the managerial ladder in terms of status. They were typically found in most specialist technical areas.

Finally, Cliques seemed to form around the Gatekeepers or within areas of technical specialisation. The field executives were one such group brought together by the common cause of running the units and the day-to-day issues that emanated from them.

Overall, I have found that corporate politics can be either constructive or destructive depending on the character of the person involved. There is no set way of identifying the key players listed. Often it is simply a question of being aware of the types of politician (as above) and intuition. However, I have found that it is worth identifying these people and seeking information from them whilst at the same time being careful about how the information outlets and personalities are handled and managed.

The situation with regard to office politicians is fluid, constantly changing and needs to be reviewed constantly. However, a person with AS is not naturally inclined or able to identify these people. Indeed, in the past I have been largely oblivious to the influence that some people can exert or of the interpersonal relationships and dynamics that go on between them.

Now, I try to ensure that I consider different people so that I am aware of what politics is operating, where the power resides, the important people I need to be talking to, the groups that they are forming and what the possible consequences are for me personally, especially so given my condition.

Above all, I have come to learn that I can never ignore or discount corporate politics. As somebody with AS, and consequently weaker interpersonal (political) skills, I need to be acutely aware of the importance, potential influence and impact of corporate politics. I have also come to appreciate the enormous advantages brought about by understanding and utilising corporate politics positively.

## Key development points

- Make understanding corporate politics a high priority. Understand and appreciate what it actually involves, what are the potential consequences and how such politics may impact on you.

- Look for, understand and appreciate where the power resides within your organisation. Be sensitive to it and the people who exercise it and try to ensure that it works to your advantage by forming relationships with these people. Utilise power constructively by adding your expertise to the sources of that power to protect and augment your position.

- Evaluate your colleagues, their positions and influence. Identify the Opinion Formers and Gatekeepers and ensure that you work with, not against, them.

- Watch political developments carefully. Be continually sensitive to the effects of corporate politics and its potential consequences, especially in relation to you.

- View corporate politics positively as something that can be turned to your advantage via positive engagement and utilisation.

# 7 Managing People

I started to work with my staff. Neil was tremendously enthusiastic and had struck up a very good rapport with many of his young counterparts at our suppliers. They saw in him the antithesis of the rest of the company, and he would spend a lot of time out and about with them.

On my first day, Neil suggested that we went for a drink after work during which he mentioned that he had applied for my job. I was aware of this, as George had told me. We had a convivial chat and Neil seemed keen to work with me. In turn, I reiterated to him that I knew little about promotional work and would have to rely on him to a large degree in that area.

However, back at the office opinion about Neil was mixed. Though widely regarded as talented, he was also viewed as something of a 'loose cannon'. One staff member remarked that though Neil was very good and well-liked, he was never around and could never be found when wanted.

My predecessor, Roger, felt similarly, though took more personal responsibility: 'I have been too soft with Neil.' I was also aware that some of the field executives had been unhappy about him, in particular about the way that he was sending 'must do' directives to the unit managers, many of which had come indirectly from the suppliers. I decided that I needed to rein Neil back a little.

The comment made to me by one of the field executives, about the department not being held in high esteem, soon became more apparent. Roger, in his final months, had let things slip somewhat. The managers' marketing scheme had been largely neglected and was nine months behind. No one within the department had shown any interest in it. Neil had disowned it, preferring instead to concentrate on more glamorous tasks and meeting suppliers. I decided to give it my immediate attention.

One day in the office I received a phone call from Bill complaining that Neil had gone ahead and implemented something without informing the field: 'This is the second time that your department has gone ahead and not informed us of things.' His manner was irate and confrontational and I did not approve of this approach. It also ruffled me. It was not the first time that he had rung up to complain, something that I felt he had no right to do, particularly in this manner. As a consequence, I reacted in an agitated way, and did not make any attempt to defend Neil.

However, at that stage nothing that Bill had said or done had really bothered me significantly. I was, though, agitated by what I saw as his continual interference and bleating. Consequently, my attitude towards him became one of indifference. My responses lacked composure or respect much as his did towards me.

With hindsight, it may have been a case of Bill laying down the law and 'putting an arrow across my bow', as if to say: 'I am someone important around here'. At the time, however, I did not appreciate or understand that. In my eyes Bill was unjustifiably challenging me and, to someone with AS, that was unfair. The politics or sensitivities of the actual situation did not come into my thinking. Consequently, my reaction was not measured, controlled, a careful defence of my territory; rather, I gave the impression that I could be dictated too easily. Unbeknown to me, I had offended an Important Other, something that was to have serious consequences going forward.

### Count to ten and do not react

It is a common trait for someone with AS to become anxious when confronted. I find that when someone is being critical of me, or when I come under pressure, I have tended to overreact and not retain my composure. This is particularly so if I feel the criticism is unjust and unwarranted. My first feeling is a physiological one: I feel tense, anxious, nervous and even frightened (as I had at the earlier mentioned crunch meeting with the divisional director), though not from a physical perspective. In many cases this has induced a knee-jerk, excessive reaction.

However, I believe that reacting in this way has rarely served a constructive purpose and ultimately has undermined and lessened my standing and gravitas. Reacting, I have found, exacerbates a problem; I gain more respect and achieve more desired results if my response is measured and self-control is retained.

Mentally, I have learnt to try and condition myself not to react when I have come under pressure. Instead I enquire as to what is actually the problem – as opposed to the feeling and personality behind it – and then try to address that problem calmly, constructively and assertively. I try to build empathy. Putting myself in the shoes of others is something that I have had to learn to do, but found to be beneficial.

As someone with AS who tends to feel emotional about certain issues, my reactions have often inflated something out of proportion and consequently agitated people unintentionally. Without being indifferent or ignoring the cause of complaint, I now simply try to care less from a personal perspective so as to avoid bringing emotion into the equation and thereby making a problem greater than it actually is. I have also come to appreciate the importance of not retaining resentment towards someone afterwards.

In the example above, my reaction had sent a clear signal to Bill that I was sensitive and susceptible to criticism. The incident also highlighted the effect any reaction can have on staff. Though I recognised he was at fault, I had not, as Neil's boss, defended him. I had failed to back him in front of others, instead of firmly but constructively managing the situation by acknowledging Bill's concerns and speaking to Neil privately later. I had sent a negative message to a fellow executive, and lost some credibility with Neil, and with it, an element of trust of a subordinate.

Over time my relationship with Neil started to decline. He began to work more distantly from me, not inform me of what he was doing or consult or defer to me for an opinion. Work was going directly to George without coming to me for approval beforehand. It came to a head at a reception one evening, when Neil accused me of being selfish and of disregarding other people. After a conciliatory meeting with George, however, the situation was resolved and we worked well together thereafter.

During my time with the leisure company I was to directly manage five other people well and developed a strong rapport with each of them. Central to this success, and to my subsequent improved relationship with Neil, was a more sensitive, openly supportive approach towards people and a greater appreciation of the need to empathise.

Although Neil needed managing more assertively and with greater control, my initial approach towards him had been authoritative, rather than assertively supportive. By empathising with people and taking a more constructive and conciliatory approach whenever there is the need to criticise, I have learnt to be able to make a point and achieve improved results whilst also retaining authority and the support of subordinates.

Changing my own approach towards people has been as much to do with generating better relations with staff as with staff changing themselves! Fundamental to this is the need to proactively engage with people and openly approach them (contrary to the normal approach of someone with AS). By recognising the need to actively manage people I have greatly improved my management skills.

Meanwhile, Helen, my secretary, was working away quietly in the background. She was a temp and was interested in staying permanently and making a career within the industry. As Roger had spoken well of her, I was keen to keep her and discussed it with George. We agreed that I should request a small pay rise and get her title changed slightly to reflect her qualifications. The personnel executive, however, was not overly enthusiastic and expressed concern that the lines of demarcation were being tampered with. It did not worry me so much: I had George's backing.

Though Helen's performance initially was excellent and she quickly got on top of the initial job tasks, her reputation both within and outside the company over time came into question. Disquiet was increasingly forthcoming about her attitude towards people and complaints became more and more common.

Initially I put this down to events in her private life that provided an understandable explanation and so I tried to defend her. Gradually, however, the complaints not only failed to go away, but actually increased. Instead of asking myself why and confronting the issue, I neglected it and tried to persuade myself that it was unimportant and would go away. Over time, however, her demeanour became more and more indifferent and though I noticed it, the warning bells did not fully register or prompt me to act.

Eventually I was instructed by Bill (by then a director), that I had to instigate a formal process and the situation concluded in a disciplinary meeting. Though the outcome was that the message was impressed upon Helen, and the issue resolved, the exercise did nothing for my stature or that of my department.

My failure to manage proactively was the cause of many of the difficulties with Helen. Because she was competent in the basic tasks that she was doing I was happy to leave her alone and – in my eyes – show confidence in her by not interfering. Whilst my allowing Helen to get on with things without interruption was indeed showing faith in her abilities, I was failing to recognise her shortcomings in some areas and also failing to empathise and supply sufficient emotional support.

The reality was that Helen needed more support and reassurance than she indicated or than was apparent to me. In addition, her self-perception of her standing within the department led her to believe that her role was of little significance. By being left to her own devices, and her motivation being allowed to fall, her perceived sense of value decreased and with it her self-esteem, morale and subsequent performance.

Unwittingly, my AS had been a contributory factor in the situation with Helen. As a result of my insularity I had not observed closely, nor been sensitive to, Helen's change in demeanour over time. Nor had I tried to empathise with it or her position. With hindsight, Helen's morale had declined steadily and I had failed to understand and appreciate this. Moreover, I had also allowed her to feel undervalued within the department and, as her manager, had not acted to redress the situation.

Generally speaking, largely because my insular nature meant I was distancing myself from them, I had not made managing staff a high priority. I have come to appreciate more than ever that it is, and the higher up the managerial ladder I progress the more I appreciate its importance. This is particularly true for a person with AS who is less naturally aware of, or interested in, interpersonal issues. Overall, my condition has brought a number of factors to bear in this area.

First, I have found that my natural insularity and independence mean that I am less likely to communicate easily and effectively with others. Second, my weaker social skills and more limited ability to empathise mean that I need to work harder to understand and communicate with others.

There is no one correct way to manage people and each person will have their own style and ways of doing so. From my experience of dealing with staff, I have drawn, as a person with AS, the following insights from some of the difficulties that I have encountered.

To begin with I believe that my actual and perceived distance has created caution among subordinates. In the feedback that I have received from staff, all have commented on how approachable I am. I am regarded as open and as someone to whom they can talk. However, many have stated that I do not naturally seek to approach them. If contact is made, more often than not it has been at their instigation.

The point about mixing with and managing others proactively came out very strongly later when I attended a 360 degree feedback course, where subordinates, peers and my superior answered questions about my management style and general work.

My boss, with whom I had developed a closer relationship than with my peers, scored me higher. In general, however, I was regarded as insular within the office. In addition, my subordinates reported that my management style was hands-off, something which the feedback from the course said was fine provided I was working with people confident of their own abilities and capable of working under their own initiative. With those who were less so, a greater degree of attention was required. Out of twenty-five managers, I was the only one who was scored as having a managerial style that was virtually totally hands-off.

My management style and philosophy have always been to allow staff to work independently, which shows – I believe – trust and confidence in them by allowing them to get on with their own job with minimum interference. My only proviso is that should there be anything that someone is unhappy about or needs assistance with, I should be informed immediately.

## Be conspicuous and communicate

Withdrawing from contact with others is, of course, natural for someone with AS. But it is also largely inappropriate in a managerial position. Today, I ensure that I pay much closer attention to the needs of individual staff and try to be more sensitive to each of their differing needs and requirements. To assist with this, I make an effort to be more conspicuous. I interact proactively with staff, as opposed to waiting for them to approach to me. I try to consider what their needs are on an ongoing basis.

I also make a conscious effort to mix. I try to spend at least one lunchtime a week with my colleagues, to sit and talk and make contact.

I also make going to out to work social events a priority and try not to miss them. Mixing with colleagues out of hours and talking about non-work-related issues has greatly helped to formulate partnerships and reduce barriers and misunderstandings with them. Finding common areas of interest for discussion is something I have found to be a useful tool for socialising!

By building rather than neglecting relationships, I have found that people are more amenable to requests for help when times become difficult.

Today I make building empathy with and understanding of staff one of my highest management priorities. I have become aware of the need to make concerted, ongoing efforts to empathise with those around me and to make more time to afford staff personal attention. Among the things I always try to do when managing people are:

- Make and find time for staff, if necessary on a regular basis. Following the investigative meeting with Helen, I instigated daily meetings with the department which, in effect, increased and guaranteed contact with all staff.

- Involve staff in issues and make sure that they feel involved and valued. I actively seek their thoughts and feedback so as to try and induce a sense of greater involvement via the regular meetings that occur, unless there is a very strong reason for them not to.

- Pay and maintain close attention. This has not been a natural inclination, given my outlook, hence the need to attach greater priority to it. Staff have, on occasion, questioned whether I have been truly listening to what they are saying! The need to do so, in order to ensure that they believe that I am receptive to them and their work, I now regard as paramount.

- Set clear objectives for people and make sure that they know what those objectives are, and support them to achieve them.

- Build empathy. I make strenuous efforts to understand things from another individual's perspective. The more limited ability of a person with AS to 'mind read' makes this far from easy but I have found it to be tremendously beneficial. If necessary, I undertake the work that a subordinate does so that I can gain a better understanding of what it involves, in order to understand them and earn their respect. I watch carefully what my staff do and how they are behaving over time. I pay close attention to their actions and I am prepared to act decisively by intervening if things are not progressing as required.

By implementing these actions and measures I have rejuvenated and radically improved my management of staff and my relations with them. I have come to firmly and passionately believe that the best way to manage staff is to empathise with people, support them and strive to ensure that I work together with them.

I have come to enjoy and develop a real confidence in managing people and find it one of the most rewarding aspects of management. Though it is harder for a person with AS, I have proved that it can be done. Today, I regard the management of staff to be one of my most important priorities and duties, and the benefits are immeasurable! As George once presciently said to me: 'A manager is only as good as the staff around him will allow him to be.'

## Key development points

- Make managing and motivating staff your number one priority.

- Manage and communicate with individuals proactively. Actively observe, evaluate and gauge their demeanour and performance on an ongoing basis. Communicate quickly and decisively if a situation changes unfavourably.

- Empathise with, and act sensitively when dealing with, subordinates. Seek to understand their position, role and circumstances to provide support and motivation by building relationships with them so as to reduce distance.

- Actively seek and maintain regular contact with others. Instigate interaction with staff to proactively build communication and trust and reduce barriers.

- Manage staff differently on an individual basis and tailor your people management accordingly. Consider what approach and actions are distinct and best for them as individuals.

- Retain self-control when challenged and criticised. Do not react emotionally and seek to locate the central issue.

- Do not regard criticism as a personal issue. Once over, let it pass and do not harbour resentment.

# 8 Forming Relationships and Building Credibility Fast

Workwise I was really enjoying the job. I was in a fun industry, I was working with colleagues that I liked and for a boss who gave me confidence, I respected and who was a tremendous mentor.

The work that I was undertaking was relatively undemanding intellectually and I was working well within the parameters that had existed in the company previously. I was not unduly concerned about this. Though I believed that major changes were needed to the marketing function, the organisational culture pretty much precluded this happening in anything other than a superficial way. If nothing else, the resources were unlikely to be available and I did not want to rock the boat, having found some stability and a role that seemed so suitable for me. I was not likely to either; it was not my style to be openly confrontational.

As time went on I tried to challenge the under-developed marketing situation as I saw it. I suggested to George that we do some basic market research around one of the units to gain a clearer understanding of the consumers who were visiting them. Business school had taught me to start with identifying consumer needs, and research was the starting point for that. But George rejected it, claiming that we knew most of this already. I did not believe we did. Most of the 'marketing' work that was being undertaken was not really marketing at all, or at least, not in the sense that I understood it. In short, marketing was not being conducted the way I believed it should!

A few months into the job I was required to work closely with Bill on a major project. A competitor was opening a complex close to an existing operation of ours that was within Bill's region. The MD had requested that we put together a response, meaning that it was especially important.

I met with Bill and travelled down to the unit to discuss the situation and put together a plan of action. We chatted on the way and had what seemed to be an easy-going conversation. Whilst at the complex Bill was clearly in charge. The manager – one of his subordinates – was present and Bill controlled the discussion. As the junior executive on his 'patch', I thought it best (and felt naturally comfortable with) allowing him to take the lead and so maintained a reserved approach.

My insularity, and natural inclination to remain within myself until I felt comfortable with a situation meant, however, that I was hesitant about becoming overtly involved, as I was unsure of my standing on Bill's territory, even though it was a marketing project and I was the person responsible for marketing. By the end of the day we had formulated a plan, much of which was at Bill's instigation; as the senior executive, he had the final say. The day ended with Bill and I parting amicably.

## Get the momentum going: be proactive

My introversion has sometimes meant that I have had a tendency to stand back initially and not project myself sufficiently in situations when there has been a need to. The instance with Bill was one example. The result is that I have unintentionally conveyed a negative impression by appearing to lack initiative or willingness to assume responsibility. Partly this has been due to a difficulty in fully expressing myself before I have built a rapport with an individual.

The best way that I have found to avoid becoming a point of criticism is to be proactive and busy and be seen to deliver. This does not necessarily involve delivering ground-breaking results. It means being active and being seen to contribute so as to establish credibility quickly in the first place.

In addition, during my time with the leisure company there were things that I believed should have been done and that I could have been doing, but because of my condition, I was reticent about advocating and subsequently delivering. My introversion has meant that, to some degree, I have been slow to take responsibility for things or publicise and promulgate my inner thinking and ideas.

Now I do not worry too much about producing the perfect solution. I simply make a start, do things and ensure that I am seen to be contributing and delivering something. I have also come to appreciate the need to advocate assertively those things that I firmly believe in.

Once every two months the managing director would have an executive conference that was usually held at a country house hotel. These were largely superficial affairs which I did not enjoy as I felt uncomfortable with the formality of the occasions and nervous and unsure about how to project myself.

In addition, I was uncomfortable being the newcomer among established colleagues, and felt some apprehension about being outside of my usual environment and in a group setting. This was something that I had always felt, but I had not previously needed to attend many similar situations. As I had with Bill whilst working on the major project, I largely kept my own counsel.

With hindsight, I prepared inadequately for these meetings and failed to utilise sufficiently the opportunity to make a positive, conspicuous contribution. As a consequence, another learning point for me has been recognition of the need for thorough preparation for meetings in order to communicate my views. Executive conferences were high profile: all executives and senior management were there and it was an important opportunity to project myself positively to make a favourable impression.

In addition, they were also political gatherings and I was not always sufficiently aware of the sensitivities of the type of subjects that I initiated. On one occasion I brought up an issue that caused some friction when, with hindsight, it would have been better to have discussed it with individuals privately.

After I had been with the company for a year, the managing director announced that he would be taking early retirement. There was therefore going to be a change at the top and, almost inevitably with it, a change in corporate direction. The new man – Geoff – seemed a reasonable person and came with a reputation of being so. However, it soon became clear that people were being evaluated and this made me feel apprehensive. It meant that I would have to gain the approval of a new person having just settled into a new regime.

Change did indeed come quickly. One executive, who the MD disliked personally, apparently as a result of past dealings, was soon dismissed. I was largely out of the direct fray, however. Coming under the auspice of George, the marketing department was seen largely as his fiefdom and his stature meant that making changes within it would be difficult for me. The new MD, however, was starting to ask questions about the role of the marketing department. In addition, he queried a couple of activities that made me feel uncertain.

I was unhappy with the situation and did not feel 'on board', something which because of my AS, made me anxious. I wanted to address this issue by speaking to Geoff on a one-to-one basis, but this was difficult as direct contact was rare. I also felt hindered, as my loyalty to George meant that I was unwilling to approach the MD directly to air my concerns.

I was concerned that with other changes taking effect, my position was under the spotlight; I realised I should clarify my role with George but was unsure how to go about it.

I broached the subject of my role and duties carefully at a meeting with George, as I was aware that he viewed marketing as very much his area. It became clear that I should play safe, not take any risks and remain loyal to him. Shortly afterwards it was announced that a new marketing manager, Terry, was going to be appointed. I was to continue reporting to George, whilst Terry was to report directly to the MD above me.

I was frustrated that despite having tried to connect with the new MD because of my concerns, I had failed, and a conflict of interest had occurred between my position and my loyalty to George.

## Establish immediate credibility

As with Bill whilst working on the marketing plan at his regional unit, I had failed to establish sufficient credibility quickly with the new MD. A core factor in this equation had been my introversion and the lack of comfort that I had felt when faced with a new situation and personality.

I have found that over time I usually come to terms effectively with new environments, tasks and individuals. However, often this has been at the cost of my losing stature initially; in a corporate context, I have learnt of the importance of establishing credibility immediately.

Now when faced with new situations, superiors or projects I make a concerted effort to negate my introversion and ensure that I connect, contribute and/or effectively communicate. In the case of a project this may involve making additional efforts to research and identify activities and solutions; with an individual, to actively engage and establish dialogue with them from an early stage.

These contributions need not be totally comprehensive; nevertheless, some sort of contribution is important to ensure that I do not allow my natural inclination to maintain distance create the impression that I am lacking confidence or effectiveness.

Shortly before Terry's arrival, a meeting between myself, Bill and one of the unit managers was arranged to discuss the marketing and sales situation within the company. All was going well and amicably until I made a point about marketing that I felt the company should be doing. The proposition was not contentious in any way.

Bill suddenly flew off the handle and began chastising me in personal terms; he proceeded to rubbish my work and express concern as to what the new MD thought of me. He also mentioned the project that we had worked on together at his regional unit and claimed that he had done everything.

I was badly shaken and taken aback by this verbal attack, though the shock of it hit me hard later. I had had no idea that Bill had such a problem with me personally and could see no reason why he should feel so strongly. I felt the outburst, in front of one of the unit managers, was particularly uncalled for and unfair on a junior executive.

My obvious upset meant that the unit manager was later asked by George what had happened: his opinion was that it had been 'over the top'. George's advice to me was: 'If I was in your shoes I would go and have a beer with Bill.' I did not see why I should; in my eyes I had done nothing wrong.

## Personal antagonism and conflict

The incident with Bill impressed upon me strongly for the first time in a work context that I had, albeit unconsciously, affronted someone as a consequence largely of the effects of having AS. A serious problem had developed between Bill and myself, although I had had no idea that he felt so negatively disposed towards me.

Ideally, the best course of action would have been to prevent the situation reaching breakdown in the first place; but it appeared past that point. It had already happened, not least of all due to the fact that I, through ignorance, had been unaware of the dynamics of the politics and of the impact of my disdain towards someone who did not share my views or sense of what was right.

But it was also more than that. According to a colleague, I had assumed the role of scapegoat as a means of enabling Bill to pass the blame.

This did provide an explanation for Bill's behaviour and demeanour towards me, and indicated that I had not been the cause of the problem originally; however, my initial reaction to his criticisms was not conciliatory and perhaps less than tactful and had exacerbated the situation.

I have come to appreciate that as a person with AS who is introverted and comes across as 'different' I am more susceptible than most to being targeted for criticism. I also understand that, because of my values and my sense of fairness and of right and wrong, my demeanour towards others of whom I disapprove can be a contributory and inflammatory factor. It is probably unreasonable, certainly contentious and possibly even dangerous to take a dislike to someone simply because I disagree with their values or approach.

I had bottled up my feelings about the situation with Bill and not confronted it, hoping that it would go away. By my adopting an 'avoidance strategy', the problem festered, and this damaged me not only professionally but also emotionally. A clear wrong, I felt, had been done to me;

but by not addressing the issue, I remained embittered by it for a long time. My AS meant that this feeling was exacerbated as my sense of righteousness had been damaged!

The problem with Bill should, however, have been faced, no matter how unpleasant or uncomfortable the consequences. As a person with AS, I am likely to feel uneasy with this, but I have learnt from experience that the consequences from both a work and personal perspective can be very serious if the problem is not dealt with.

I felt that my lack of seniority meant that confronting the problem would be risky. But it should have been done and it would have given me a better chance of protecting my position in the long run. The key issue was to approach the problem in the correct manner.

Jane Clarke, in *Office Politics*, identifies two facts that are essential for conflict resolution. The first is a real desire to solve the problem. The second is to view the situation objectively – even if it is personal – and to approach the situation in a way that focuses on solving the problem.

In the case with Bill, I eventually came to have a very real desire to solve the difficulty. Deep down I did not really dislike Bill personally; indeed, I had much respect for him professionally. The problem was the second factor: I objected to the way that Bill ran other people down and deflected criticism onto them as a means of protecting himself. I believe he had no right to act this way, and that it is a very serious issue.

Hard though it is for a person with AS to accept, it is important to acknowledge that these situations will arise in any workplace from time to time. I now question candidly whether I have in any way contributed to the ill feeling of another person, and I demand that I am honest with myself about this. But I also believe that not to stand up for myself when someone is challenging me unfairly, as Bill did, is to invite trouble: something I no longer accept.

Unfortunately, it quickly became clear that Bill did not just dislike me but did so greatly. It seriously affected my confidence, partly because of his high standing within the company but also because all the other field executives – with whom I got on very well – were aware of his views too. It was a situation that was to have ongoing, serious consequences for my role and career.

Some of the cause of my problems, however, had lain in my approach to Bill and my general approach overall in the early stages of my joining the company. To begin with, as a person with AS, I had naturally shown little interest in issues and relationships outside of my immediate department. I had assumed that these were of little relevance to me and had not tried to proactively build relationships with a wider circle of executives. The need to do so was an important lesson learnt and was certainly so in the case with Bill. By reacting towards his pressure initially I had antagonised a colleague, and an important one at that, and failed to build a relationship with a significant figure.

Second, because of my natural introversion I had not projected myself adequately to my colleagues, or at important events such as executive conferences when there was the opportunity to build my profile. In effect my views and inner thoughts were discussed mainly between myself and immediate superior and I did not share them sufficiently with a wider audience. Consequently, my fellow executives, who had not worked in marketing, failed to understand the rationale that underpinned my thinking and actions, or appreciate my considerable skills in the area. In addition, my natural inclination to keep important knowledge and thinking to myself until I felt totally assured had projected an impression of my being inactive and ineffective. I have since realised that many of my ideas were correct, but I failed to promote them sufficiently. The need to express and promulgate my thoughts and views quickly and consistently is something that I have now come to appreciate as vitally important.

### Sell yourself

As a person with AS I have learnt of the need to promote my work and myself – something that does not come naturally to me. I am by nature introverted and relatively indifferent to what goes on around me; I also tend to assume that I will automatically receive credit where credit is due and that people will notice, understand and appreciate what I am doing. My experience has taught me clearly that this is very rarely the case.

Throughout my career I have not publicised and promoted my achievements – of which there have been many – sufficiently. Now I promote myself and publicise my achievements widely. I use all available opportunities, whether it is management meetings, internal newsletters, or one-to-one meetings to communicate my actions and achievements. If I do not, then no one else will, so I make it one of my key priorities to ensure that everyone knows what I am doing and the value of it.

Technically I was doing my job very ably. I had assumed responsibility for the department and I was operating competently and effectively. I successfully marketed new openings, implemented a number of promotions (one alone earned the company £100,000), and I ran the department professionally.

My list of achievements was considerable, but I still felt that my position was susceptible, as I was not operating in the way I believed I should be. My abilities and notable achievements would effectively mitigate the difficulties faced as a result of my AS as I was going forward significantly.

## Key development points

- Communicate your thoughts and promulgate your views conspicuously. Advocate what you believe in and ensure that you are always contributing.

- Build your profile and credibility with each individual, especially those at the top, quickly and proactively. View new situations and first contacts with people as an opportunity to project yourself and create a positive first impression.

- Develop relationships with colleagues outside of your immediate circle. View them as potential sources of assistance and support. Communicate your views and beliefs to secure consensus and support going forward.

- Watch your reactions, and be respectful to others, in particular those who do not share your views or sense of values, so as to avoid possible provocation. Make a special effort to be amenable towards those of whom initially you do not approve.

- Be sensitive to, and confront immediately, any predatory actions by others against you. Approach the situation objectively and communicate your concerns assertively.

- Sell and promote yourself constantly and publicise your achievements! Utilise both formal and informal channels such as meetings and face-to-face discussions to promulgate your views, objectives, actions and achievements.

# 9 Honesty, Trust, Assertiveness and...Business

In his book *Asperger's Syndrome: A Guide for Parents and Professionals*, Tony Attwood identifies being 'honest to a fault' as a key trait of a person with AS. According to Attwood, people with AS find it necessary to be totally honest when expressing their views. This is due in part to their highly developed sense of right and wrong, but also to their inability to locate hidden meaning in interactions.

The need to be honest and frank is something that I have always adhered to throughout my life and, in general, I believe it to be a beneficial trait within a business context. However, there are times when, with hindsight, I believe that my being too open and willing to engage others frankly has brought difficulties. The need to be more guarded and, at times, reserved, is an important lesson I have learned and one that has guided me away from potential pitfalls.

A key source of income for the leisure company was its discounted ticket scheme whereby tickets were sold up front at a discount to organisations and used as promotional incentives. Over the years thousands of tickets had been sold this way and the company had accrued significant revenue as a result. Promoting and selling them vigorously was therefore advantageous for me.

An opportunity arose to run a promotion in one business sector with a company that were to use the tickets to incentivize young customers to purchase their products. At the very time that I began to arrange the promotion, my company was negotiating to become involved in a larger, national scheme with a number of our competitors a year later. If this scheme came to pass, it would mean being unable to formulate any indigenous promotions ourselves within the same sector in the following year.

Until the last minute it remained uncertain whether we would participate in the national scheme, however, as numerous hurdles had to be negotiated. To compound matters, one of our major competitors was undertaking a bespoke promotion of their own, earning large amounts of revenue and generating enormous publicity; and George was stating that we had to 'protect our business'. This added to the pressure on me to respond.

As the current promotion that we were running independently was coming to an end, the agency who had originally instigated it requested that it be repeated the following year. I was unsure. If the national promotion came to pass we would be unable to do so. If it did not, however, we would want to continue to enjoy the revenue stream that resulted from the local promotion. I needed to cover all the options. Imprudently, I did not refer the issue to higher management and, as the idea of the national promotion seemed to be collapsing, I resumed discussions with the promotions agency who were pushing hard to re-sign.

Instead of saying no to their request 'until further notice', I prevaricated and agreed to continue supplying tickets in the medium term. These tickets were to be used in a larger promotion that was due to run for a further year, and the promotions company, unbeknown to me, had assured their client of a supply for that period. Unfortunately, the national promotion that we were negotiating suddenly came to fruition, meaning that we would be unable to guarantee further supply of tickets to the client after all.

This became a very problematic situation, one that took careful negotiation and work to resolve. The base line was that I had been too accommodating towards the agency and insufficiently businesslike when negotiating with a third party. I had also failed to empathise sufficiently by putting myself in the situation of the third party. The incident impressed on me the need to retain distance when negotiating and of not trying too hard to accommodate or please.

## Trying too hard to please and saying no

I enjoy helping people and dislike confrontation. My natural inclination is to try to please people and accommodate them. However, my difficulty in saying no, and my less developed ability to effectively 'mind read' have occasionally led me into difficult situations when dealing with others. I have not adequately questioned or gauged others' motives, and I am less likely to say no, as confronting difficult situations and making unpleasant decisions are things that I do not find easy.

The case with the promotions agency was such an example. They had an agenda that was at odds with that of my organisation and I had not sufficiently evaluated the position from their perspective or considered the consequences. By trying to please and be amenable, I had created a problem.

In his book *Making Friends: A Guide to Getting Along with People* Andrew Matthews advises people wanting to say no to: keep calm and authoritative; not offend; continue to use the same words when stating your case; be persistent. He advocates not to be defensive or apologetic, but to simply state matter-of-factly that you cannot do something at this point in time and, that if you do, it will negatively impact on your other work. I heed this advice and action it when I need to.

Now, if I find myself being pressured to do something at a particular time, being cajoled to say yes, or trying to automatically please, I put a mental brake on proceedings, and ask myself if my actions are likely to cause any difficulties to my own position and that of the company.

I have found a useful tactic is to delay by asking for more time to consider; but ultimately, if I have to, I am not afraid to say no.

Another issue that I have had to learn to guard against is my tendency to be too honest and open towards others. An example of this came with the closure of one of our older units, a subject that was always sensitive given that many of the company's operations were elderly and had been part of a town's tapestry for a considerable period of time. The local population was, therefore, often understandably opposed to their closure.

My company had developed a new unit in the town adjacent to where an especially old unit had been operating. Past experience had taught us that the impact of this would be highly negative, making the operation of the older unit untenable and the performance of the new unit suboptimal. The decision was made to close the old unit.

A local newspaper began a campaign to save the old unit. A journalist called enquiring as to the reason for its closure. Whilst expressing sympathy and understanding towards the town and its occupants, I stated that it was unrealistic to keep the old unit trading, and explained the effect that the new unit would have on the old. The journalist subsequently misrepresented my words in print, claiming that the decision to close was not ultimately necessary.

### 'Honest to a fault'

The example of the unit closure and my dealings with the journalist high-lighted my honesty when dealing with a third party, along with my desire to act with the best of intentions. Though these traits are common to a person with AS they are not always appropriate within the business world, and in this instance had got me into deep water.

Among the lessons I have learnt are not to divulge too much information, nor to feel compelled to give reasons for not wanting or not being able to do something. This approach does not mean being dishonest; nor does it mean being 'economical with the truth'. More accurately, it means being careful about the information disclosed.

As well as guarding very carefully against my tendency to be open and completely honest, I am also mindful that not everybody else is entirely honest or in possession of the degree of integrity in their dealings within a business context as I believe and expect they should be. I have also learnt to question very carefully others' motives and intentions in business dealings.

Moreover, the higher up the managerial ladder I go, the greater the stakes and consequences, and the more imperative the requirement to exercise caution and care when dealing with others.

Exercising these guidelines has again brought real benefits for me and helped to prevent me getting into difficult situations. They have also helped me to learn how to deal effectively with others, enabling me to gain considerable confidence and assuredness as a result.

## Key development points

- Be cautious about trying too hard to please others within a business context. Be fair but firm in dealings with others, and do not promise anything other than you can realistically deliver. Do not agree to things over and above what is required from your perspective and that of your company.

- Guard against being too open and totally honest. Be careful about how much information you disclose.

- Question what others are telling you: do not automatically accept at face value what is being presented.

- Be aware of the views and motives of others. Ask yourself what are their requirements: do they conflict with my interests or those of my company?

- If you have to, be assertive and say no!

# 10 Confronting Issues

Within the company, George's retirement was imminent and thoughts began to focus on what would happen when this occurred. The feeling was that Terry would move up from marketing manager to become the head of marketing. What would happen to me was uncertain.

I was getting on pretty well with Terry. However, he had gained a reputation of lacking tact and had upset a number of people both inside and outside of the company. Murmurs started to circulate about the MD's relationship with him. The latter had appointed him and they had worked closely at a previous subsidiary together, so why would he not support him? The feeling was they were not getting on and George alluded to it. I, however, had not sensed anything; my AS had meant that I had not picked up on this, and so was unaware of what was happening in the wider context.

A memo soon circulated to all executives announcing that Terry had decided to leave the firm and pursue opportunities elsewhere, as he had been unable to pursue his career the way he had wanted inside the company. To me it was a shock, but it presented an opportunity to re-establish my position as the most senior marketing person.

The next question was, what would happen to me now? The answer was that nobody really knew. On George's retirement it was announced that Bill would be promoted and that the field executives would report to him. There was no mention of what would happen to me or the marketing department.

After a long delay one of the field executives casually mentioned that I had a new boss! Apparently, the MD had announced at a meeting that I would be reporting to him, as Bill's responsibilities did not include marketing. The official line was that with his other duties it was too much for him to have responsibility for marketing as well.

The real reason, which was confirmed privately later, was that Bill had refused to have me report to him. The situation was far from ideal as I would inevitably still have to work closely with him. As the MD's right-hand man, he would impart significant influence. This situation reinforced my feeling of isolation and distance from the executive team.

The good thing was that the change meant I would report directly to the MD and so be able to build a closer relationship and argue my case more effectively with him. An appraisal followed and we spoke openly. I conveyed to him the concerns that I had about my previous lack of direct communication and inability to project my real views.

I received a very favourable and understanding appraisal. It complimented me on some promotions and recognised that I had had a difficult year with a new marketing manager being appointed, but that I had supported the new person during his short time with the company. The MD also clarified my tasks for the foreseeable future.

The recognition of loyalty was important, as was the clarity of position, as it meant the frustrations that I had been enduring previously had been acknowledged. In addition, I felt that I had gained some respect, if not yet the total confidence of the new MD. My morale improved greatly!

After a year of working with Geoff I had a further appraisal. Rather than a straightforward one-to-one discussion, all executives went through a new process where a manager and his superior would answer a questionnaire to identify what both parties perceived to be their strong and weak points. This would then identify areas for improvement and those tasks that were essential to advance each department and area function. The final part was a discussion between manager and subordinate to discuss, identify and agree on the best way forward, along with timescales.

It was an excellent methodology and when I sat down with Geoff to discuss my plan we had a thorough discussion of the areas for personal and departmental advancement. It was agreed that I could have the additional member of staff that I had long been requesting, and other key objectives were agreed.

I was on a high, as I felt the uncertainty that had been on my shoulders for a long time had finally been lifted. I had been given clear objectives, ones that I believed could make a real contribution to the company and which would enable me to utilise my specific insights and analytical skills and demonstrate what I could do. What was more, I had been given clear timescales in which to achieve them. There was no more uncertainty with my role or position for at least six months; I could relax and get on with it and I was up for it.

## Clarify the issues: get clear guidelines and instructions

Another common trait of AS – allied to a dislike of change – is the anxiety caused by uncertainty. I find it unnerving and uncomfortable when I am unsure of what direction I am going in, what my duties and responsibilities are and, in particular, if I feel that a superior is unsure about me or what I should be doing.

In short, I like clarity and a structure. I find that if I am comfortable in my role and I know what is expected of me and where I am going, I am able to relax, become motivated and able to fully express my abilities and fulfil my capabilities. To enable this, I endeavour to make sure that my tasks and responsibilities are clearly identified and, if necessary, written down. I make sure that everything is clearly understood by all parties, especially the person to whom I am accountable. I also ensure that I feed back to them via open lines of communication.

Ideally this should be in the form of regular one-to-one meetings. If this scenario cannot be secured, I try to ensure that I communicate regularly by other means – e-mail or written memo, for example – and keep copies of correspondence relating to particularly important issues as a future reference point. I ensure that any issues of uncertainty are clarified quickly and that all work and achievements are effectively communicated.

One of my tasks included evaluating a marketing loyalty scheme. Another was to formulate marketing plans for three new retail openings, one of which was very high profile and necessitated working alongside colleagues from the other subsidiaries. In addition, it was Geoff's personal project, one that he had fought for and instigated, so would be a chance to personally shine. I was excited and motivated by the prospect.

A meeting was called by Geoff with representatives of the other three subsidiaries and an action plan agreed. One executive – Norman – was a young, ambitious manager, looking to personally progress.

The first task was to appoint an advertising agency who would be responsible for the launch under our direction. In order to brief potential agencies an initial selection screening was to be arranged within seven days. All material was to be submitted to me for distribution to the various agencies. The instructions and requirements were clear and explicit and everyone agreed to them.

I received what was required from one manager within a couple of days but Norman did not deliver. Despite a number of approaches to him none were acknowledged or responded to. Consequently, I was obliged to call Geoff to tell him, only to be informed that it was not a concern and that we would 'talk again on Monday'. Happy that the MD knew why I had not been able to complete the task to the timescale outlined, and that it was beyond my control, I was able to leave the matter.

On Monday morning, however, the situation had changed. I received a letter from the MD informing me that the project was to be passed over to Norman and his team. I was very displeased. Not only had one of my key projects been taken away from me, it had been done through no fault of my own and passed to the very person who had failed to honour his responsibilities: this seemed unfair. I felt that the MD was questioning my capability.

In fact, there were sound reasons for giving the project to the subsidiary company to manage. Norman had project managed and opened similar sites before and had significantly more human resources and expertise to support him. It was also a highly political project where failure to deliver would have enormous repercussions. But, if the MD felt that way, why had he given me the project in the first place?

## Managing your boss
## and defending your position

The introversion inherent in AS often results in a reluctance to face issues of an interpersonal nature. Though I was getting on well with Geoff and had formed an acceptable working relationship with him, I had not impressed myself sufficiently on him. He still did not fully understand or appreciate what I required from a personal perspective, or what needed to be done professionally.

My AS, though a natural barrier, should not have precluded the need to actively manage my personal situation and position. I should have taken responsibility for the situation constructively and made my views known. Even though he was MD, Geoff was not interested in the marketing department and had, in essence, neglected it. But as the person responsible for it, I should have ensured that he did show an interest, and made my views known; or, as Jane Clarke points out, it was up to me to: 'demand what you are entitled to'.

Experience has taught me it is imperative to request what I require. On occasions I would discuss 'concepts' with Geoff, and for the most part he was reasonable and would listen, but he did not appreciate marketing issues, and was not interested in addressing them. Consequently, I would get a negative or unenthusiastic response. It was frustrating to encounter such a barrier, but I realise that I also failed to sufficiently elevate the importance of issues via discussion documents or similar to promulgate my views.

I do this now, and I believe it is essential to be seen as proactive so as to enable me to say 'I have advocated these things'. I later regretted that I had not formally presented my clear and passionate views of the marketing requirements of the company. I also believe that I should have fought more vigorously for the things that I knew to be right.

Now I regard as vital the formalising of my thought processes and beliefs. Doing so raises my profile and promotes and covers my position. If I cannot realise the essential things to enhance and protect my position, then I may need to make the decision to change it. Now, I am unwilling to remain in a position where my duties and input can be questioned and challenged.

I called the MD and enquired why he had changed his mind. He prevaricated and was non-committal, but essentially said that Norman had the better support. I then called Norman and asked him for his view of the situation: 'That is something that you will have to discuss with your boss.' I did not ask him why he had not supplied the information he was asked, and indeed obliged, to.

## Challenge people

Because of my unease with, and natural inclination to steer away from, potential conflict, I have often not reproached people when it was necessary and when I would have been justified in doing so. It is essential and I have learnt to do so much to my benefit.

How I deal with people, and my ability to challenge them if required, depends very much on the attitude I encounter. If a person responds constructively and honestly with me, I find I can argue my case vigorously with them. If, on the other hand, I suspect that they are acting in an underhand way or are not seriously interested in discussing something constructively, then I find it difficult.

However, I now refuse to allow something to go unchallenged if I believe it to be unjustified or unfair. Nor will I allow a situation to pass that may reflect poorly in turn on me.

I should have challenged Norman and done so using facts by formally communicating to him that I was unhappy with the situation and why, and then done likewise with my boss. In cases such as this, by not accepting things at face value and questioning them further in a constructive way if necessary, I have acquired the ability to retain greater control over situations and acquire higher respect and stature as a result.

My morale and motivation were adversely affected by the incident, which forced me to give the situation a lot of thought. Where was I going to go from here? More pointedly, with Bill in the position he was, was there realistically any chance of progressing further within the company? The more I thought about it, the more I came to the conclusion that there was not. I decided I needed to move on.

I started to put out a few enquiries in the industry, but after some initial efforts to secure alternative employment, eased back. As there appeared to be no immediate threat to my situation or position, I decided to stay put! Besides, I liked the job and was content not to have to face change that was, of course, adverse to my natural inclinations. In short, though I had made a decision, my love of, and comfort with, routine meant I had not followed it through.

I began to work on my other appraisal tasks, one of which was to launch the new units. The first marketing exercise was to hold a 'ground-breaking' ceremony to start the project, and gain some important initial publicity by announcing to the town and surrounding area that the unit was on its way.

The exercise was very simple and low-key. A dignitary, usually the mayor of the town, was invited, followed by a photo-call on the site that would appear in the local paper. The radio station in the town would also attend, and the local 'movers and shakers' nurtured.

I arranged the ceremony in Bristol. All went well and then I had to do Leeds, so started to implement the same programme. I sent a memo to all the participants clearly outlining what was required of them, and confirmed that they had received and understood the correspondence. All confirmed that they had – and did – including Jim, the technical manager, who had done the same simple thing before, and was a senior executive. There was no reason to anticipate any problems.

I called all three participants again a week before the event, to check that they were all OK, and whether there was anything else that I needed to do for them. All, including Jim, confirmed that there was not.

The day before the event I made one final check by calling everyone to ensure that there had been no final, sudden problems. All again confirmed that there were not, including Jim, who I spoke to personally. I had written to everyone and made regular checks up to and including the day before. Everything was watertight and there was nothing more that I needed to do.

Prior to leaving the office at the end of the day I received a call from Bill expressing concern about the morning's event and questioning whether everything had been arranged properly. I did not understand. Everything had been, as I knew, having just spoken to all participants who had confirmed they understood their responsibilities and that there were no problems. I was therefore confident that I had covered everything. I was puzzled therefore why Bill should be concerned or why he was calling.

However, when I turned up at the site the next day, all hell broke loose and Bill threatened my personal existence. Jim had told him that he had no idea what he was supposed to be doing, and Bill had immediately assumed that that was the case. There was no question of asking me for my side of the story, no questioning why Jim was there if he did not know what he was supposed to be doing. Instead, a 'major catastrophe' had occurred and, in Bill's eyes, it was all my fault.

In the event, everything went well and worked perfectly. Nothing happened to cause any embarrassment for our guests but that was not what got reported. Back at head office, Bill was going around making out that it was a disaster, with the guests having been embarrassed and the company put in a highly degrading light. Moreover, there was no doubt as to who was to blame for it!

The fallout was severe, and I was unsure about what to do. I tried to minimise in my mind the damage that was being done to me personally, my reputation and standing. The whole thing was inexplicable and nonsensical, and I simply could not comprehend what Jim had done, why it had happened and, therefore, relate to it.

Shortly after I was called up to Bill's office to discuss another matter. The atmosphere was tense. At the end I broached the subject and apologised for the events of a few days past, but said that I had been let down very badly.

It did not seem to register with Bill. He was sorry too but, 'I cannot stand seeing the company being put in a bad light'. It was still my fault. What's more, Jim had told him that if only I had called him the day before, he could have done something. This was nonsense as, of course, I had. Jim was not telling the truth; but I did not challenge Bill or defend myself sufficiently, and the failure to do so was to cause me enormous anger and frustration later.

The real issue, though, was Bill's personal dislike of me, which meant I was wary about taking the subject further because of the consequences, as I was a junior executive and therefore in a position of weakness. However, the central point was that I had done nothing wrong.

## Face down the problem

The issue with Bill had reached crunch point and should have been faced, but the problem was I unsure how to go about doing so. I did not want to have to confront someone who clearly disliked me, something that, due to my AS, I was both apprehensive about and ill-equipped to do. However, this, and the magnitude of the problem, made it imperative that I should have.

Jane Clarke's first point in dealing with a conflict situation is to ensure that you choose any battles carefully and for the right reasons. The key to this is to ask what the impact will be if the issue is not addressed. For me, in my position, the answer was clear. Bill was doing terminal damage to my position, and our poor relationship was detrimental to the corporate good. This alone made facing the issue justifiable and necessary. Of additional pertinence was the fact that I had been personally threatened.

When dealing with such a problem, Clarke again provides a useful framework:

- Be specific.
- Make sure that the place is appropriate.
- Do not delay.
- Put the effort in to prepare properly.
- Anticipate the response.
- Balance positive and negative feedback.
- Deliver negative feedback in a non-critical way.
- Concentrate on the pitch and tone so as to deliver in a non-complaint mode.
- Beware of patronising.
- Remember throughout that the aim is to solve the problem.
- Dealing with a problem is affected by the type of person being dealt with. This needs to be evaluated carefully.

This, I believe, I should have done in the case of Bill, and done so in the presence of the managing director. I had done nothing wrong and should have used the facts and evidence, such as memorandums and the back up of other participants, to prove it.

One of the most worrying findings of research into Asperger Syndrome has been that the condition triggers a predatory reaction in certain people (Attwood 1998). This was, I believe, what happened in the case with Bill. It is a very serious potentiality and one that I now guard against very carefully.

Experience has taught me the imperative of not allowing myself to be victimised. As a person with AS, I am conscious that my introversion provides the possibility that I could be attacked personally and made a scapegoat. Though it is hard to confront such issues, I regard it as essential to do so. Bill's demeanour towards me was totally unacceptable and I had the right not to tolerate it, and to be treated fairly.

When the chief executive, whose personal style had permeated the whole organisation, retired after many years, there was a change of personnel on the main board. We were all called (as previously mentioned) to a meeting with the new divisional director first thing one Monday morning.

His first words to me: 'Yes, but what about the consumer?' caused me to come away from the meeting worried and concerned. This man was not going to sit back and let the current management run the company independently. He was going to get involved personally and it would not necessarily be in a consensual fashion.

I called Geoff to discuss my role, and the current approach of the marketing department, as I believed it was open to question. The MD himself was as concerned as everybody else and unsure as to the best approach. Suddenly, however, there was a surge of interest in the marketing department: the additional member of staff I had long been requesting was finally and belatedly approved, along with another person, a talented young manager in creative design from the field.

Shortly afterwards, I was informed by the MD that a Marketing Director was to be appointed. Our conversation ended with Geoff saying that he thought I would feel better as a result.

### Being a number two

The interpersonal skills of someone with AS means that being exposed to politics can be highly stressful. Throughout my career I have found that simply doing what I am required to do and not having to become embroiled in interpersonal politics makes me feel more comfortable. Though I seek increasingly senior positions I have concluded that holding a senior Number Two position may be for me a better option!

In such a position I have found that I am far more likely to grow and develop, and will encounter less upheaval or exposure to politics or situations that require strong interpersonal/political skills. Moreover, working for and supporting a manager is something that I enjoy and find rewarding.

The decision depends on personal viewpoint and circumstance but, if it is that I am more comfortable as a Number Two, then I consider it very carefully, and do not allow myself to think that my not pushing for higher positions demonstrates a lack of ambition or ability. If that is what is right for me within an organisation, I accept it and avoid the anxiety of being in a position that exposes me to unnecessary stress.

Against that I also felt somewhat let down. I had asked for my position to be clarified and it had not been. None of the directors had shown any real interest in the marketing department and whilst all the other departments had been given additional resources, I had been given none, despite my requests.

The net effect was that my standing over time had diminished and my position had become untenable. In effect, my career within the company had stagnated and gone past the point of retrieval. The decision that I had come to earlier about looking for another position had been the correct one and, with hindsight, I should have followed it through.

## When the need arises – change

A preference for routine and a dislike of change are key facets of Asperger Syndrome. These factors have sometimes delayed my changing roles or moving on. Central to this is my natural inclination to preserve what I know, such as a situation that I have come to feel comfortable in. However, I have learnt that my preference for routine and aversion to change must not prevent me facing decisions if my situation indicates that change is needed, as there comes a point in all careers when this is the case.

By being open to change and welcoming it, as opposed to fearing it, I have been able to make progress in my career and in my own personal development. I have also become increasingly comfortable with change, something that has greatly enhanced my confidence!

I was then told I was to see the new divisional director again for a further meeting. I felt unable to be totally frank or speak my mind about things as they currently stood, and told Geoff so prior to the meeting. However, I was told if things got 'heavy', he (Geoff) would handle it. In return I requested that I be able to discuss the company's branding.

The need to change this – or 're-position', in marketing parlance – had been a strong personal belief based on my MBA training, but one that the MD had dismissed. The company enjoyed a very high profile and its name was instantly recognisable. But it was a name that was also resonant with the past and was regarded, in my opinion, as staid and tired by our young, core audience.

Though the company was highly profitable, its market share was slipping and had been doing so for a long time. Fundamentally, the business had been starved of investment and a new, fresh image that repositioned the company in the eyes of consumers was required to give it a real chance of competing with the new, modern entrants.

The idea was more radical than anything that had been done, or even contemplated, in the field of marketing within the company in the past. My key analytical and strategic skills enabled me to see the wider, more important picture. In my view, it was essential and needed to pre-date any other marketing activity as it was the brand, its positioning and the image that stemmed from it that would act as the base for any further marketing and promotional activity. The problem was, was that the directors did not understand it. The MD agreed, however, that I could bring up the subject with the divisional director and, as I had his agreement, I felt happy and able to do so.

I presented to the divisional director. He listened attentively and we engaged in what seemed like positive discussion. The session lasted over three hours and ended with my explaining my views on the branding issue. I left feeling relieved as well as satisfied. I felt that the meeting had gone quite well, that I had performed respectably and that I had not let down my boss.

However, there was to be change, and it came about very quickly. A new managing director was to take over in the New Year and Geoff was to be moved sideways. Soon after, it was announced that a new marketing director would be appointed for a short period. The new man – Ray – was a highly experienced marketing professional, described by the new MD as 'brilliant'. He was mature as well and that, allied to the fact that he was only going to stay for a short period of time, was reassuring.

Meanwhile, I was told I was to meet Geoff who was to inform me what my pay award was going to be, as it was his duty to do so prior to handing over his responsibilities. I was hopeful that it would be positive. I had spoken to him about this previously, as I knew that there was going to be a review, and he had said that he would be considering an increase. However, this was not the case: I was informed that I would not be getting any pay rise at all, due to underperformance!

The examples given of my underperformance were spurious. The criticisms levelled against me were unfair, inaccurate and unjustified and the way that Geoff treated me hit me personally. I had grown close to him in the two years that I had worked for him and had grown to like and trust him. Others shared the view that this was unfair. The opinion of the personnel officer was that I had been treated appallingly and made the scapegoat.

### It's business!

As with most other people with AS, my sense of loyalty is innate and pronounced. I felt a strong degree of loyalty towards Geoff and believed that it was justifiable to expect it from him and others to whom I had shown it myself.

However, I have come to realise that it is unrealistic to expect reciprocal loyalty in a business context. Changing circumstances, different managerial preferences and business strategies all mean that individual positions are inevitably transient.

Having – in my eyes – my loyalty disregarded by Geoff was a painful personal experience but another invaluable lesson: that in business, I cannot automatically expect from others what I regard as fair treatment.

Today, in order to protect myself and my feelings, I do not expect loyalty from superiors, no matter how closely I work with them, or how highly I regard them. Circumstances, I believe, dictate that it cannot be guaranteed or presumed.

I no longer regard it as being disloyal if I feel that an organisation cannot support me, or if things are not moving in a way that is beneficial to my career or situation. This can include having to work under someone whose management and personality I cannot accept. I have come to understand that I need to consider myself first. If a company or a manager is not demonstrating a commitment to and support for my position, then I do not regard it as an obligation to feel committed and unquestionably loyal in return.

I was told to prepare a presentation to provide the new MD and marketing director with an overview of the company's marketing situation. I worked hard on the preparation for this and it went well. The new MD was receptive and interested in what I had to say, and there were no really difficult spots.

In the meantime, Ray started to talk to people about their views of their roles and whether they wanted to move to the new head office. We discussed my position and I was asked if I was interested in the role of marketing director. I informed Ray of my background in the company and what had happened with Geoff, but I refrained from mentioning my relationship with Bill.

A few days later I heard from Ray that the company was not, after all, willing to offer me the marketing director position. He also told me that any middle-management roles that were available were at a lower level and probably demeaning for me. He insinuated, too, that Bill had been highly critical and unsupportive of me. I decided to look for another position outside the company.

The day I left, I received a private and confidential letter from the new MD thanking me for all my efforts for the company over the previous five years and wishing me every success in the future. None of the other executives who were leaving received one – only me!

It was a sad day when I left. My confidence was adversely affected as a result of the experience and, though the new MD's complimentary letter had encouraged me, I had lost a job that meant an enormous amount and I was now out of work.

However, with hindsight, the upheavals that I went through during my time with the leisure company provided some invaluable lessons for the future – lessons that were to contribute hugely to my future progress. These included the importance of always arguing for, and striving to secure, what I believe in to protect and enhance my position.

Soon after I left the organisation, Ray instigated a revised corporate identity – a re-branding – the very same thing that I had believed was necessary and had argued for unsuccessfully. This, among other events within the company, confirmed that my thinking had been correct and that in the future I could have the confidence to advocate strongly what I understood to be right. Most importantly, my experiences impressed upon me that some of the obstacles that my condition presented were not insuperable and could not prevent me from succeeding or realising my full potential.

## Key development points

- Clarify your objectives and ensure that your lines of responsibility and personal direction are clear. Formalise them and communicate your progress to superiors continually.

- Proactively manage your superior by constructively asserting your status and responsibilities. Ensure that he/she understands what is required of you and what you need to achieve it in terms of resources, support and working conditions.

- Fight hard for what you genuinely believe in, and promulgate your views so as to protect and enhance your position. Do not allow your introversion to prevent you from effectively doing this. Communicate your opinions consistently both formally and informally – verbally, in written form and visually, by presentations – to ensure that your message is heard. Ensure that your unique skills and different insights and ways of thinking contribute fully, and add to, debate.

- Be decisive and assertive to ensure that you can justify your job task confidently, and that your position is not exposed to unwarranted criticism. Avoid assuming a position that you do not personally believe in or could not feel able to advocate and defend.

- If something or someone's actions are not right, question and challenge them by using facts and avoid bringing personal criticism or dislike into the process. Do not allow yourself to be a scapegoat.

- If a relationship problem is serious, and you are being personally denigrated, confront it! Do not allow anyone to victimise you. As with unacceptable or questionable actions, confront the issue objectively using facts.

- Be loyal but do not expect automatic loyalty or the complete trust of anyone in return. Maintain distance in dealings with colleagues and remember that relationships are business, not personally, orientated.

- Consider whether a situation is beneficial and advantageous to you and do not allow personal loyalty to block your own advance or sustain you in a disadvantageous or potentially detrimental position. Respect your own interests as well as those of your superior.

- Learn to accept and engage with change. Identify the time to move on so as to progress and maintain the learning process. Do not allow aversion to change to block personal and professional progression.

# 11 If You Meet 'That' Person

My next role was with a small company which represented a number of professional services firms nationally. To begin with I was not given any objectives nor was I sure exactly what I was supposed to be doing other than 'generating some profile (publicity)', so I started to use my initiative. My past experience meant I was determined to be proactive and to do what I thought was right and should be doing. If nothing else, I was going to build a position that I could personally defend if challenged and questioned.

I read around the subject and produced a strategy paper which I presented to the MD. It was viewed very favourably internally and it provided him with a strategic direction that could be worked towards. It also provided him with some support as he had complained that he was doing too much himself.

I generated some 'profile' for which I gained further credit, but to gain further publicity I needed the tools to achieve it and so asked to assume responsibility for a piece of publicity recruitment material that had been commissioned by the MD. The company had not recruited members for a number of years even though there had been plenty of enquiries, and in fact was actually losing them. This raised my suspicion that all was not well or quite what it seemed within the organisation.

I discussed the publicity material project with Alan, the MD, and got permission to proceed with a series of regional meetings. The firm would shortly be ready to go out and actually recruit new members for the first time in a long while.

I was beginning to enjoy the role, particularly working within a small firm where I could work under my own steam, something that suited my style and personal working requirements. The company certainly thought that I was delivering. I was told by the MD that colleagues were talking about how much I was doing and how I was beginning to make things happen.

At the regional meetings, I did a presentation based on my strategy paper. It went well. I set out my stall clearly and argued my case convincingly, including at the last meeting where a great deal of the discontent among the membership was manifested.

I received nothing but praise later from the MD about my performance. He also informed me that a former director, who had attended as an ordinary member, had called to say how impressed he was with what I had presented. He had congratulated the MD on his choice of marketing manager, and finished by saying 'You have got the right person doing your marketing there.' Apparently, it was unheard of for this person to offer such praise.

Shortly afterwards the MD mentioned that there would be an additional non-executive director joining the company in a marketing/sales capacity. I was told that the new director, Tom, was mature, semi-retired and had been a highly successful salesman. My immediate thought was of being able to work with an experienced, avuncular figure along the lines of George and Ray and from whom I could learn. I looked forward to it.

When I met Tom briefly, following his arrival, he was not what I was expecting. He was elderly, and his attitude was cold, distant, unfriendly and stand-offish. It made me suspicious.

My initial impression was confirmed shortly afterwards at the next managers' meeting. The finance director started to voice an opinion but was immediately interrupted by Tom with the comment, 'Well, you don't need to do that.' His manner was dismissive, contemptuous and confrontational.

I immediately sensed that this man was going to be difficult, both by what he said and the way in which he said it. It seemed he was trying to put people down and dismiss any viewpoint, rather than constructively engage and challenge people's thoughts or opinions to prompt debate. It was as though he was setting out to deliberately subjugate people.

Although I could not substantiate it then, I felt there was something disreputable about Tom, about his personality, his manner and the way that he was likely to act. It was as if there was something almost fraudulent about him, and I made up my mind immediately that I disliked him, though I did not know exactly why.

My intuition told me that there was a big problem up ahead, so when asked my opinion outside by Jim, my closest colleague, I could not help but reply that Tom was 'going to be real trouble!'

My colleagues seemed initially unconcerned, but I was not. I was becoming aware that my feeling towards Tom heralded a potential problem, one that can be insuperable for someone with AS: that is, the difficulty of relating to a person whose actions you view as unjustified and unacceptable.

A second round of regional meetings also went very well and impressed members were asking for copies of my presentation. Afterwards, during dinner one evening, the MD expressed the view that my support was influential in him wanting to stay with the company, as he had been contemplating leaving.

Back in the office, Tom was meeting everyone and asking people what they were doing. During my meeting with him I explained the publicity work and showed him the results that I had generated. I discussed the new membership, explained how the company had not recruited new members for over four years and described what I had done to get the project moving. His reply seemed dismissive of my efforts to identify and recruit new members, which I found confusing, as it seemed to me that we should be taking the initiative in this area.

I felt as though he was playing games with me, trying to unsettle and undermine me, rather than challenging me in a positive, constructive manner. It is likely that he was testing my resolve, gauging my reaction, but because of my AS I failed to recognise this or respond appropriately. I felt unnerved by what seemed an illogical criticism of my exceptional results. I also disliked the way he was acting as a manager, and I objected to the way he was belittling people. My initial suspicions of Tom and his motives were reinforced.

I asked why he was joining us and what his background was. He replied that he specialised in 'turnaround situations' and our meeting ended with him saying that he thought that it was a 'super little company with wonderful products'. I felt that our meeting had gone quite well and that he had not caused me any trouble personally.

Indeed he had not. Though I was highly suspicious of him, Tom had done nothing at that stage to actually offend or damage me; neither had I done anything to offend him (or at least, not as far as I was aware). Nor had I done anything to undermine his authority, been insubordinate or refused to do anything. I did think, though, that he expected people to be subservient, almost reverential, towards him and saw no reason to do that. What was more, I was not going to!

## Avoid being judgemental

People with AS often have strong principles and tend to have rigid and keenly held values and moral standards. Certainly I believe this is the case with me. When people with AS encounter a person who seems to hold completely contrasting principles to their own, there is a danger that they will become most inflexible and uncompromising, and capable of affronting and antagonising the other person.

Now when I meet a person who induces a strong negative feeling in me because of their different moral principles, I try not to be immediately judgemental. I challenge myself about the opinion that I have formed of the person concerned, and ask myself whether this person has actually done anything that causes me personal difficulty. I also consider what it is that has specifically offended me. In short, is my interpretation justified?

I challenge myself further still to try and accommodate what has happened, and reduce the level of personal feeling by trying to alter my perception of that person. Does what happened really matter? Downplaying the importance of the issue to me personally takes the emotion and seriousness out of the situation, and therefore reduces its potential to anger me.

Though I now make a conscious effort to smooth the path of relationships by being conciliatory and amenable towards people whose personal demeanour contradicts my expectations, there are some instances where, for a person with AS, this is particularly difficult.

The heightened sense of right and wrong of someone with AS, coupled with the sensitivity that both parties have vis-à-vis their own values and behaviour being challenged, can make for a volatile cocktail. This may be further exacerbated as the lack of empathy, distance or formality that someone with AS demonstrates towards people whose values differ may be perceived as obstinacy or insubordination.

There is another factor to consider. What one person regards as morally acceptable behaviour may be regarded as highly unacceptable by another. However, this may be their way of acting and they may believe it to be correct, particularly if certain circumstances justify it. In the situation with Tom I had failed to take into account the politics and business scenario that related to his behaviour: I simply did not want to. I had formed a negative opinion about Tom and was not prepared to give him the benefit of the doubt.

## The Fundamental Attribution Error

The Fundamental Attribution Error is described as the tendency to attribute the 'unacceptable' actions of a person to their internal disposition or personal traits, as opposed to the environment or circumstances that they find themselves in.

It is regarded as an error because such an interpretation often involves underestimating the impact of the external environment and places excessive and even unfair responsibility for the behaviour on individual traits or tendencies. Instead, a person may be acting in such a way as a result of circumstances or the effect that those circumstances necessitate or place upon them. Such behaviour may be significantly different from that which that person would normally demonstrate.

At first Tom's approach seemed at odds with that which would have been expected, given the story that the employees had been told: namely, that he was coming in on an advisory basis, to add experience to the company. Though I immediately disliked his behaviour, and was suspicious of his motives, I did not try to reason why he acted as he did.

If I had questioned and understood the reasoning behind Tom's employment beforehand, I *may* have inferred earlier that something serious was afoot, that his demeanour and actions had a purpose and that he had real authority. As a consequence, I *may* have felt less emotional about him. He was, as Bill had been at the leisure company, an Important Other and one with whom, whether I liked it or not, I would have to forge a relationship if I wanted to retain my position within the company in any meaningful form.

There was also Tom's background. He was a salesman. Salesmen sell. By implication they are assertive operators whose objective is, as Tom would say many times over the next few months, to 'hit the figures'. Nothing else is of importance, as that is their job. If salesmen do not succeed they are shown the door. All blunt, but that is the reality of the situation: there is no room for friendship or sentimentality.

A good salesman may also twist a situation a bit, talk it up. His job is to sell and if that means exaggerating a benefit and being slightly economical with the truth, then that is justified and considered acceptable practice to secure a sale. However, being anything other than totally ethical and honest is, of course, contrary to the thinking of someone with AS.

I had not considered the situation from any of these perspectives, nor had I considered any of the related factors. Emotion had overpowered my thinking and made me act in a way that was likely to be extremely pro-vocative, given Tom's authoritative outlook. The alarm bells rang for me about Tom but I did not fully consider the consequences of my judgement or actions.

Unexpectedly, it was announced that the finance director was leaving. Senior within the company, he had considerable weight. However, it soon became apparent that the finances were in bad shape and that Tom had orchestrated his removal.

Tom was becoming increasingly bombastic and disrespectful towards other employees, claiming that the MD was doing everything, and implying that people were not pulling their weight.

I did not like this. I was not sitting back doing nothing, I was getting on and doing things: for example, Tom had identified the selling of products to the members as a priority and Alan suggested I take on this task, as one who 'got things done'. I also felt I was providing the MD with the support that was a factor in his decision to stay on. Tom could not, therefore, reproach me, and I had decided that he was not going to!

## Challenges to the self-concept

Something that can also incite a negative reaction in people with AS is for their concept of themselves as individuals to be questioned. I have found that any assertion that challenges my perception of my 'self-concept' can induce a strong emotional reaction. I dislike anyone regarding me as something other than I understand myself to be. Central to this is my high integrity, honesty and sense of fairness.

Now, if I receive any challenge to what I regard as my 'self-concept' I immediately ask myself whether I have the right to dismiss automatically the view of the other person and try to be more flexible in my interpretation. If I believe that their challenge is unjustified then I approach the matter constructively: is it something that is worth getting heated about? If I can, I change my perception and interpretation and seek to discuss the issue with the person concerned, so that they understand my concerns.

I had little contact with Tom until one day when I entered the office to see him talking to another member of staff. I walked past without acknowledging him and went and sat at my desk. Within moments he approached me and asked whether I had done a particular task – something minor and unrelated to the main tasks that I had been given. I was not, therefore, working on it. I replied that I had not, but before I could explain further he flew off the handle and started shouting me down loudly in front of all the other staff about not doing my job, and then walked off. Later the same morning at the managers' meeting I was shouted down again and accused of not doing a different task I had been set. A person later commented that, 'Tom was pretty strong with you.'

Tom clearly had picked up on my dislike of him and had implemented his favourite 'put someone down' tactic: namely, asking a question about a low-priority task which, not being done, gave him the pretext to shout a person down for not doing their job. To me, that was unethical and I objected to it. My initial feelings about Tom were being confirmed to me; or had I provoked him?

Over time a number of other people also started to object to the way that Tom was treating them. The IT Manager in particular seemed to be a target and was being attacked very personally. People were becoming increasingly disillusioned and were looking for, and acquiring, alternative jobs. As time went on Tom's negative comments and criticisms increased, and his general demeanour deteriorated even further. People were being openly berated and castigated and morale in the building was falling rapidly.

Personally it was simply confirming what I had thought of Tom from the moment he arrived and first spoke. At best, I found his management totally demotivating, at worst, depressing. He would not offer any form of advice and you could not even be sure what exactly he wanted, such was the conflicting nature of his comments and actions. If asked something he would not respond, and he would fail to give an answer as to what exactly he required. His management style was distant, non-collegiate and focused, as he would say, only on business. It was therefore at odds with the supportive, inclusive style sought and required by someone with AS.

In addition, to my mind, he was morally hypocritical. Though he was quick to berate people and accuse them of not doing things, he seemed unable to actually do things himself. Instead he would pass on contentious tasks that were his responsibility to other staff whom he had previously criticised as slacking. When one person refused to do the task he requested they were dressed down and grossly humiliated via the same tactic of being asked an unanswerable question.

I had reached the stage where I felt that I could go no further. I had been tasked, and was under pressure, to get revenue in; I had done so and, when I had produced the goods, had simply been belittled and dismissed by management. I went to see the MD and asked if I could have my appraisal brought forward as I needed to clarify the situation. I was conscious of what Alan thought of me personally and the value that he placed on my support for him. As the person who had taken me on I felt he deserved my loyalty; in addition, I felt a degree of responsibility to him.

My intention was to have a frank and honest conversation with him and explain that, though he appreciated what I had done, I could not tolerate the situation – or more accurately, Tom – much longer. However, Alan was busy and I had no option but to leave it until after my impending holiday, when we could discuss the matter.

One week before I was due to go away all employees were called into the management meeting room to be addressed by the Chairman. The news was not good. It transpired that the company was in very bad financial shape. To use the words of the Chairman: 'If we carry on like this we are going to hit the buffers.' There was a serious financial crisis, which the company had tried to keep a secret because of the possibility that it could have terminal consequences if the members – already largely dissatisfied – found out.

Upon my return from holiday I found that Alan had resigned due to stress. Tom had assumed complete control with immediate effect: an outcome that meant my position was untenable. Things within the company were also coming to a head and the situation was apparently critical. I was dismissed immediately by Tom for spurious reasons, including the expenditure on the new membership promotional material that Alan had instigated and approved after I had asked to take over responsibility. I was given no opportunity to respond, and Tom had not discussed my position with the other managers, knowing that they were positively disposed towards me: this meant that he could then act unilaterally.

Tom's behaviour, to my mind, was unacceptable. However, though he had not added any form of value to the company's operations, the decisive action that he instigated to cut costs had saved the company from demise in the short term: was that not the most important thing? However, to this day I still find it impossible to accept the tactics he deployed and the way he treated people in the process.

My intuition had told me from the moment that Tom first spoke that I was not going to be able to work with him. There were characteristics of his personality that were completely irreconcilable with those of a person with AS. My perception of his personality included:

- a cold, distant, unfriendly approach to people

- a style based wholly on 'business results' without consideration for personal feelings or circumstances with no margin for error or licence

- a non-collegiate, unsupportive, critical style of management

- a less than honest, manipulative style and manner

- hypocrisy: the inability to do himself what he accused others of not doing

- a bullying demeanour

- unethical behaviour.

In other words, my perception of Tom's character from the perspective of values and moral principles was such that I was never going to so much as try to accept him. The difficulties that subsequently developed with Tom were largely due to traits inherent within my AS that made forming an effective relationship with him impossible and therefore my subsequent reaction and approach to Tom made conflict inevitable. The fact that others came round to concurring with my viewpoint of Tom had no impact on my personal outcome. The power in the situation resided with Tom, meaning that my stance of outwardly refusing to accept his behaviour or pander to his ego was dangerously counterproductive.

However, though the experience at the time proved to be a negative one in the short term, I was again able to draw invaluable lessons from it that ultimately proved to be highly beneficial in the future.

First, I have learnt that, as a senior manager, it is important to ensure that my personal feelings and moral perspective are not part of a business relationship. My dealings with Tom highlighted the need for this clearly. Now I make a concerted effort to understand and relate to people such as Tom, who have initially triggered my suspicion and moral disapproval. This positive approach has brought me immense benefits and has literally transformed my dealings with certain people, turning potentially hazardous situations into positive ones.

Discovering this ability has contributed enormously to my self-confidence in dealing with people and has encouraged me to work on my interpersonal relationships further. Given that personal interactions and relationships have been the prime source of difficulties throughout my managerial career, the benefits brought by this new-found confidence in dealing with relationships are immeasurable.

Second, I do believe that people with AS are going to find it impossible to work with people such as Tom. Though the situation may be difficult for everyone, it is harder for people with AS, due to their poorer social skills and their inability to empathise with people whose moral principles are significantly different to their own. If the challenges to the principles and self-concept of the person with Asperger Syndrome are particularly severe, then the consequences are likely to be intense, even traumatic.

In this situation, I believe it is most sensible to extricate oneself immediately, thus avoiding a significantly difficult and problematic relationship. During my career I have got on well with the vast majority of people with whom I have worked. However, in those exceptional circumstances where this has not been the case, I ensure that I avoid those who are, for me, antipathetic people.

## Key development points

- If you believe that someone's approach is unethical, inducing an immediate emotional reaction in you, be careful before prematurely forming an opinion. Before you react, question your initial impression and response, particularly if there has been any challenge to your self-concept.

- Make a special, concerted effort to be accommodating towards the person. Be amenable and proactively engage with him or her, building bridges and developing empathy where you can.

- Disguise any negative personal feelings towards the person concerned and ensure that any interactions are objective and based on business-related facts and opinion only.

- Adapt emotionally to situations. This is helped by understanding the motives and objectives of others so as to provide an explanation for their actions. Identify the mutual benefits that their actions have conferred, to reduce tension.

- If the emotion induced by another is extreme and intense, question carefully whether you can build an acceptable and working relationship with that person. If, after careful consideration, your intuition tells you that this is not possible, or if the working relationship deteriorates and becomes antagonistic, extricate yourself from the situation as soon as possible.

# 12 It's Not Just What You Say

I declined the offer of garden leave and decided to work my notice period to give me time to look for another position. I did not say anything to my subordinate, Jack, the day my redundancy happened but when he asked the next day what had occurred I held a conversation privately with him.

During our conversation Jack asked me what I thought was going to happen to the firm. I replied somewhat injudiciously, saying that I did not know, but that since these situations could be so unpredictable, with some companies going bust and others going on to make millions, the best thing would be for him to keep his head down, get on with it and wait and see. My words were metaphorical, influenced by the emotion of being dismissed and my personal anger at the way I felt that I had been treated by Tom.

When Alan learnt of my redundancy he was shocked and surprised. The other redundancy that had taken place had been discussed as a group and Tom had asked Alan and other senior personnel for their thoughts on the performance and role within the company of the individual concerned. He had not asked about mine. When I told Alan that one of the reasons given for my dismissal was my spending the money on the new membership material, he responded that it was unjustifiable as that money had been budgeted for and he had agreed it. It was indeed unjustified, but of course that was not the true reason for my dismissal.

The atmosphere within the company began to deteriorate badly. People were under pressure and beginning to act irrationally, including

Tom. Jack had so offended an elderly, female employee with his comments that it induced a major reaction on her part.

I later encountered a consultant who had been out of the office for a while. He too had been targeted by Tom and was offended by his attitude. He was sorry to learn about my redundancy and commented that he felt Tom had been unfair to me. I replied that I could not work for Tom, given his style of management. My reference was to Tom's style of management, not him personally. Jack, who was sitting opposite, became involved in the conversation, and commented 'You have got to be positive.'

An hour later I was summoned to speak to Tom. He told me that he was not bothered what I said about him personally but that he objected to my bad-mouthing the company and saying it was going bust. Jack had gone to Tom and embellished the conversation that the consultant had instigated with me earlier.

When I denied the comments, particularly the assertion that I had attacked him personally, and told him that I resented the accusation, he seemed indifferent and appeared not to believe me.

I was agitated that I had been accused of making comments that I had not made, and by the way I had been portrayed. I was also offended and angry at having my integrity attacked by a person who, to my mind, had acted with little integrity himself. That Jack had twisted and taken out of context specific words that I had said to him in confidence also upset me.

## Dangerous words can be costly

As a person with AS, I find that the subject of integrity is especially important to me. It engenders powerful emotions in me, such that I am liable to express my opinions strongly to convey my values.

Though I had acted responsibly by speaking in private, my words to Jack were perhaps careless and open to misinterpretation or mischief. This was particularly so, given that I was talking to a young person and an extroverted, garrulous one at that.

Today I make an effort not to allow myself to become embroiled in loose talk or idle chat. I refrain from involving myself in gossip. Instead, I try to mind my own business, and take the view that other personal matters are nothing to do with me, however interesting the subject may appear to be.

I have come to appreciate that, because of my heightened sense of right and wrong and literal interpretation of honesty, I formulate strong views and opinions about things. Others may not share these or appreciate my expressing them openly. This means that I now guard against their expression.

In addition, I watch my language and try to select more appropriate words. Over time I have come to appreciate that my choice of vocabulary has sometimes been strong and to the point. Whilst my views about a particular subject may not have been especially controversial, the way I have communicated them may have given a misleading impression and antagonised people.

Now I temper my words and stop to ponder before I comment. I am wary of the fact that things I feel emotionally about have the potential to lead me into difficulties. Also, my strong belief that I am technically or morally right, and my tendency to speak up about something, are not without danger.

If I do need to make a point, I try hard to find words that are conciliatory and not likely to inflate or exaggerate out of proportion my views, feelings or the subject in question. In a nutshell, I ask myself: does it really concern me and, again, does it really matter? If not, I stay out of the fray and refrain from commenting!

Learning to modulate my vocabulary and select words that are appropriate to a context and setting has brought me many advantages. First, I find that I am able to communicate my objectives more effectively and in a way that conveys greater gravitas. Second, I can do so in a way that does not impinge on the views and sensitivities of others, which adds to the weight and impact of my argument.

Both of these points in turn have helped mitigate any negative personal feelings of frustration that I may experience as a result of not being able to get my message across. By communicating proactively with others in a way that takes into consideration their thoughts and interests, I have gained greater support and understanding from my colleagues.

A short while later, Tom came around the office and introduced a new managing director. Tom was leaving the company. He was leaving, to my mind, before he had seen the job through. Though he had cut the costs dramatically to return the company to short-term profit, he had not, in my opinion, addressed the strategic situation that the company had to face if it was going to survive in the medium term and beyond. This point was later expressed by the new MD and a number of members who remained dissatisfied with the terms of their membership.

Moreover, he had dismissed me unilaterally in the knowledge that he himself would be leaving a short time later; he had not discussed my position with the other managers, knowing if he did they would have supported me and advocated for my retention. The new managing director's first words to me were, 'I hear that the company has let you down!'

However, he also stated that if Tom had not cut the costs the company would not have survived. This was undoubtedly true; and ultimately, was this not the most important thing of all?

## Key development points

- Control and restrain your emotions in a corporate environment and try to ensure that personal feelings and opinions are kept separate from professional matters and relationships.

- Do not become involved in contentious areas that are of no direct concern to you. Avoid gossip and speak only about matters in which you are directly involved. If someone tries to persuade you to give an opinion about a matter that is personal or potentially inflammatory, refrain from commenting.

- Watch what you say and choose your words carefully. If you wish to make a point, do so with words that are objective and not affected by emotion. Ensure that words are temperate and do not exaggerate or inflame unnecessarily the message that you want to communicate.

# 13 Productivity and Efficiency

As well as the benefits of learning how to deal effectively with mainstream management tasks, such as managing people and understanding corporate politics, my experience has delivered significant advantages by helping me develop efficient work practices. These have brought many benefits and have also reduced related problems in other areas and greatly enhanced my overall management performance.

My redundancy from the small professional services firm meant I was facing change again. I wanted this time, therefore, to find a role that was relatively secure, in an environment that was stable. I learnt about a position within the BBC. As I had thought about the corporation before, being a settled environment, not overtly competitive, and offering wider opportunities within it, I applied and got the job.

The BBC had a distinct and unique culture. It was full of highly creative, dedicated people who were interested first and foremost in producing quality media material. In many ways it was a leviathan that operated in a set way and was subject, for better or worse, to a degree of inertia. Against that, not being subject to blunt market accountability, management looked to develop people.

After beginning in a relatively junior role I looked to move into higher positions. One came up in a central department and really appealed to me. Moreover, it was one that would enable me to utilise my MBA skills. I had an initial interview that went really well, and was called back for a second one to meet the head of the department.

I was apprehensive about the interview, partly because I was now so close to achieving the position, mainly because of the interview being conducted by the department head. He had a reputation within the organisation of being highly intelligent, but with an awkward demeanour. On paper he was the type of person that I was not sure I would feel at home with. This turned out to be correct. His manner was impatient and the atmosphere in the interview room was tense. I simply did not feel right.

The environment that I would have been working within would also have been intellectually very demanding and, more pertinently, would have called for working intellectually at speed. In the main, I could probably have done 90 per cent of the work, but not necessarily within the timescales required. Working under pressure to produce high-level work spontaneously would have put considerable pressure on me. The role was therefore not suitable for me and in the event I wasn't offered the position.

## Intellectual requirements

An important lesson that I have learnt over time as a person with AS is not to overstretch myself and to find a work level that I feel intellectually comfortable with. This is one that does not overly expose me in terms of excessive intellect or learning requirements and one that is not going to subject me to undue pressure in the short term. I have found that it is important that I have the opportunity to grow into a role and fully learn and absorb the material.

When I have learnt a job and feel comfortable within it, I find that my confidence grows disproportionately higher and faster and I am then able to excel within a position. Once I have found my feet, I then begin to become more proactive and assertive.

If I assume a role that places me in an intellectually pressurised environment initially, the subsequent anxiety prevents me from overcoming any initial hurdles. I therefore fail to acquire the knowledge and personal foundation that would enable me to flourish. In short, as with 'Being a Number Two', I am aware of my limitations and avoid positions and environments that put me in situations of undue intellectual pressure.

Shortly after, another senior role emerged. It was within a department where I had struck up a relationship with a person whilst working on a one-off project that drew on different departments across the organisation.

His help proved invaluable. Not only did his technical information contribute greatly to the presentation that I was due to give, but his inside knowledge of the department helped to guide me as to what the director was looking for – an example of good networking and the benefit of striking up a relationship and rapport with a colleague!

My colleague informed me that the director was very down-to-earth. He had been within the BBC all of his career and had worked his way up through various positions and departments. The interview went well. Derek was frank and honest, we had a good conversation and I felt comfortable with him. I was offered the job later that day.

The role proved ideal also. The department was a small one, meaning that it had a close-knit feel to it. The atmosphere was friendly and constructive which stemmed, to a large degree, from Derek's style of management. Positives were passing down from the top.

I quickly formed a very high degree of respect for him. His grasp of all aspects of the business was very sound and his style of management was inclusive and constructive. In short, it was just the type of management that I needed and responded well to.

My role was Head of Marketing and I had two junior staff reporting to me. One was relatively new, talented and an ideal staff member. The other had been at the BBC for a time and was disillusioned; I was told she could also be difficult. I looked forward, though, to managing staff once again, confident that my past experience would be beneficial.

I was also more confident about my ability to handle the job technically. My leisure experience had acted, in a way, as my apprenticeship and I would be able to put that to good use. All my past efforts and learning could be turned to my advantage. In addition, I would be able to work on some high-profile brands that would be good for my career and my CV.

The work, in effect, was publishing. Every ten days there would be a management meeting at which new, potential publishing projects would be evaluated and considered. The meetings took place in Derek's office and were informal.

A number of processes fed into the commissioning process, which overall was quite convoluted. There were issues regarding finance, sales and marketing, intellectual property and development, and each one was dependent in a way on the other. Before the intellectual property team could ascertain their costs they would need to know what material the development team would require to creatively develop the product! They, in turn, needed to know from the sales and marketing team what type of product to develop. Consequently, the commissioning meeting was in many ways a political gathering, where there were considerations of inter-departmental issues and group dynamics.

## The group phenomenon

I have always found the experience of groups difficult and they have impacted greatly upon my career, work experience and management. Consequently, I have made a concerted effort to study and analyse quite closely the dynamics and effects of groups in order to gain a better understanding of them.

A group is defined as 'when the term *we* is used, as opposed to *I*, and the properties of a group are more than the sum of its individuals' (Morgan and Thomas 1996, p.43). In theory, a group can mean two people; more often it will be three or more. In addition, a group can be either formal or informal.

This immediately indicates a challenge and potential problem for someone with AS, as groups require one to interrelate with, and consider the views of, numerous others in a dynamic setting. An understanding of the politics that goes on within a group setting is also required.

Research has highlighted a number of important factors and influences that affect, and operate within, groups. The following is not exhaustive but I have found these points to be relevant and useful to me personally:

- The views and opinions of those within groups tend to converge towards the first and most convincing viewpoint. Often this is that of the most dominant person. In addition, there is pressure towards conformity and, in general, the minority view can be a cause of social tension.

- Being considered part of the in-group is important if one is to be a successful and influential member of a group.

- Resisting the influence of the majority is not easy, particularly for an individual. A minority of two is better placed to resist the influence of a majority within a group and be able to remain independent.

- The ability of the minority to effect and exert influence is greatly diminished if a viewpoint is presented argumentatively or in a dogmatic style. A flexible style of negotiation is required, is more beneficial and is usually successful.

- Groups often have a history and a real life role and the properties of a group may well outlast individuals over time. 'Boundaries' are also present: unwritten rules that need to be respected.

- A large discrepancy between a minority view and the majority view will affect any outcome. Also of importance is the wider context beyond the immediate group; that is, whether a position is advocated that is in accord with the spirit of the times.

- Bion asserted that two agendas operate within groups: first, the overt or conscious work or primary task; and second, the 'hidden agenda' that concerns the life of the group itself and which contains intra-group tensions, relationships and emotions. The latter will function to satisfy the needs of the members and act as a defence against anxiety (Wetherell 1996).

- Bion also identified a 'collective mental activity' that emerges when people get together, even if individual members do not intend it and are unaware of it (Wetherell 1996).

I have experienced a number of the above points, particularly during my time with the leisure organisation. To start with, my introversion and natural inclination to remain insular contributed to my withdrawing and being considered as not 'on board' or part of the group. I was viewed as, and always felt, an outsider.

The effects of this position manifested themselves in other difficulties. As my subject area, marketing, was misunderstood by the majority, there was an innate suspicion and general disregard for it. As a result, I held a 'minority view' which made it even harder to get my point across or defend myself against the alternative prevailing opinion.

Overall, I failed to understand adequately the stance or feelings of others and the need to account for these when presenting material or arguing my case. As a result, I had a conscious feeling (see below) of being a focal point in conferences, which had negative outcomes for me personally.

### Group dynamics and the impact on the individual

Being part of a group also has a significant impact on and potential implications for the individual. Again, the following list is not exhaustive but I have also found these points are relevant for me as someone with AS:

- A person's self-perception when they become part of a group affects how they behave in certain situations. Thoughts and behaviours are adjusted to match the defined attributes of the social group.

- People tend to feel more comfortable if there is a consensus for the view that they are expressing. Consequently, people often undertake a process of comparing themselves with others so as to be in tune with general opinion. They will shift that opinion more easily if they believe that the in-group is similar to themselves.

- Identification with a group will elicit a tendency to conform to the in-group norm. In practice, behaviour is affected by a complex intermixture of personal influences and group identity.

- Emotion may also exist meaning that people people are less than truthful about relationships and the situations in which they find themselves and so unconsciously work to avoid personal anxiety and conflict.

- Groups can induce anxieties as unconscious feelings are transferred and conflicts re-instigated. These can be rivalries, bullying, conflict with parental figures, pressure or a lack of appreciation by influential group members or the group leader. An important source of anxiety in groups is the need to differentiate oneself and maintain a sense of identity.

- Unconscious defences operate in group settings: denial, or rejecting all difficulties; cynicism: reacting with contempt to the views of others; withdrawal from the emotional life of the group, possibly via silence; competition: feeling superior to others to avoid anxiety; and intellectualism: exercise of the intellect rather than the emotions.

- Feelings or aspects of personality can be 'projected' onto other group members. A projector can, by a variety of means, force the recipients of the projection to 'feel' and 'experience', a process known as 'communicative projective identification'. This can often result in conflict between individuals or within the group.

In addition, the above effects can lead to roles within a group whereby group members may unconsciously select one individual to hold an emotion for the group. As a result the person may become depersonalised and take on the behaviour that befits what is being projected, whilst those projecting have 'got rid of it'. This 'malign projection' can often occur where one member exhibits signs of anxiety and can lead to their becoming a victim or scapegoat who is then victimised further, subjected to ridicule and bullying, and made 'useless'.

As an insular, independent individual, and one who does not possess advanced social skills or the ability to discern the motives of others easily, a person with AS is vulnerable to these occurrences. I have experienced a number of them within group settings, along with their consequences.

To start with, I believe that my apprehension and nervousness at having to be within formal groups has been evident to the other group participants. This was particularly so in the leisure company, where the executive conferences were a regular occurrence.

My first problem there was that I had failed to build satisfactory relationships with my colleagues beforehand. As a result, I failed to get consensus and support from them. Second, I would largely withdraw from proceedings, contributing only when I had to. Usually I would seek to complete my contribution quickly instead of using it as an opportunity to advance my case and that of my department. As a result, my area received less attention and priority than others, and as a consequence, I did not develop gravitas or give an impression of effectiveness in the eyes of my colleagues.

My low profile also resulted, I believe, in my being the recipient of the negative projection as identified above. My introversion meant I presented an easy target for others within the group, something that I was aware of. As an individual, I 'held emotion'.

After I had been in a new department in the BBC for a couple of months, Derek e-mailed me to say, in his usual constructive way, that he was getting 'bad vibes' and that there was a perception that I was not fully picking up on things. He went on to say that I was retaining support because people liked me and I was seen as wanting to learn and progress. The reality of the situation, though, was that I had not yet fully grasped the underlying rationale for the material that I was working with. Part of the problem was that I was not listening actively to what was being said or fully absorbing the information, the inferences that stemmed from it and, therefore, the consequences of it.

## Learning and working under pressure

I have always found it difficult to learn whilst I am under pressure, particularly if the pressure is extreme. This is illustrated by previously outlined examples, such as working with the external consultants whilst at the retailer.

Relating the subject matter of my study to actual experience or a real life example is beneficial, but another approach I have utilised is to learn outside of the work environment or when the need to deliver results is absent. Reading around the subject and gaining as high a level as possible of technical knowledge is also important.

By making efforts to learn outside in a relaxed, unexposed setting I have found that my thought processes are clearer and my ability to learn and absorb new material improved. In addition, I try not to learn excessive amounts of new material at one go. Often I have found myself skimming over subject matter and trying to absorb large quantities of information, as opposed to taking things in a piecemeal fashion and fully understanding basic concepts (on which understanding more complex data depends), and then progressing. Slowing down my approach to tasks also assists with this process.

The best way to avoid pressure, however, is to prevent it in the first place. Particularly when I am faced with something that I am not interested in, my tendency has been to put it to one side and deal with it later. Additional pressures have then built up, meaning that, by the time I have come to face doing it, I am not relaxed and feel pressured.

Now, if something is impending I start work on it immediately and try to clear it as soon as possible, long before a deadline, if need be!

Concentration in meetings and absorbing all detail within them has also been a problem for me. Typically, I find myself drifting in and out of a discussion and thinking about unrelated matters. Temple Grandin describes this effect as 'associations' whereby her mind wanders from one subject to an association with it, to another association, and so on.

Once I have stated my case – the facts that matter to me – and I have made my contribution, I feel (often unconsciously) that I can then withdraw from the discussion. This has a number of negative consequences.

First, I find that I miss important pieces of information. Something will be said that is important to the debate and the outcome that is being determined and I will fail to pick up on it. As a result, I do not cognitively process and absorb all the facts or entirely pick up on the development and result of the debate. I have also been guilty of exacerbating the situation by later making comments that indicate that I have not fully listened to all the arguments, something that raises question marks about my attention span and credibility.

Allied to withdrawing from the discussion once I have made the points I believe to be important, is a tendency to remain insular and silent, with a limited level of input overall. I have found that it is vital in meetings to say something and make a full contribution. Failing to do so and withdrawing into my own world has given a negative impression. Now, I always ensure that I prepare fully for meetings and take them very seriously.

## Meeting preparation

As a meeting is a group phenomenon and consequently a potential source of anxiety and difficulty, I make a special effort to think ahead and prepare for it properly. Many difficulties have occurred in meetings as a result of my being insufficiently prepared from both a mental and professional perspective.

Among the contingencies I make are to think ahead and identify any possible 'hot spots' – issues that are likely to cause particular problems – and how they could impact upon me. I prepare properly in terms of my input and contribution to ensure that it is relevant and clearly presented, both verbally and in any written form. To ameliorate the problem of putting forward a minority view that may be out of sync with the thoughts of the majority, I ensure that I present only if I have a strong conviction so that I feel confident in arguing my case. Above all I try to ensure that I make some kind of positive, constructive contribution to all meetings that I attend, to achieve profile and create an impression of contributing.

I concentrate: and to assist with this in meetings I do two things. First, I make a special effort to concentrate in the first few minutes of proceedings so as to ensure that I pick up on the initial thread of the debate. Second, I take notes. I find that this not only helps to ensure that I stay involved and listen but also that I do not have to rely on my memory to recall facts later. When I do say something, I try to make eye contact with all colleagues at regular intervals during my input; I also make use of my hands to gesture and regulate my facial expressions so as to increase my level of interaction.

If I do make any comments I try to ensure they are relevant and accurate. If I am not sure about saying something, I do not; I make a conscious effort *not* to make comments unless I am absolutely certain of my facts and sure that it will make a positive contribution to proceedings. Before I do comment, I try to think through carefully and properly what I am going to say and what its impact will be both on the subject matter in question and on the others present. In order to stay involved in the debate, I also ask questions, which has the added benefit of helping me create the impression of being interested.

To defend myself against criticism, I try as far as possible to gather as much factual data as possible to support my stance. This makes it easier to substantiate any point I make and also supports any subjective arguments and insights which, as a person with AS, I may also wish to make. If criticism is forthcoming, I ensure that I consider it, acknowledge it and respond constructively in a non-emotional fashion. To help gain approval of the main issue, I look to concede smaller, more minor points and acknowledge the views of others.

I have also found that running an idea past colleagues beforehand is beneficial, particularly past the Opinion Formers and key decision-makers, and especially so if any material is contentious. This makes it less easy for a person to attack a proposal later and helps to build some form of prior consensus.

Having a communicative and constructive boss in Derek was also helpful and I received a lot of invaluable feedback from him via his open, honest support. Among his observations of my personal management style were that I tend to see things very much in 'black and white' terms and that I often jump to assertions that are based on intuition as opposed to hard facts – or alternatively, my thoughts and opinions are not supported by factual data.

## Actively consider and question
## the viewpoints and opinions of others

My tendency to see things in 'black and white' terms means that I trust and believe things I am told often without challenging them. This is another variance of being 'honest to a fault', or having a trusting and accepting nature, along with the tendency to interpret literally. On a few occasions I have automatically taken the misguided words or actions of others at face value.

Now, if something does not immediately feel right I stop and question it. I contemplate and think through the logic of any message and no longer automatically assume that the person is always correct or is acting in a straightforward, honest manner.

Allied to this, I have learnt to consider alternative viewpoints and, importantly, not to so readily dismiss the views of others. I find that my thought processes very quickly guide me to a conclusion based on intuition. Now, I challenge this also, or at least back up my arguments with supportive facts and, in addition, actively seek and consider alternative viewpoints and courses of action. The latter, in particular, I have found helps to reduce friction with colleagues by not quickly dismissing their views, leaves me less open to criticism and also gains me support going forward.

Inherent in the process of collating, evaluating and considering alternative views, options and opinions is the ability to listen. It is a skill that has been greatly under-developed with me. As well as my tendency to simply state my case and then withdraw mentally has been a basic inability (for example in meetings) to concentrate and fully absorb matter when speaking to others.

This is all part of communication, which I have come to appreciate is a two-way process. Listening is a vital skill and one which I have really had to learn.

What is listening, what does it actually consist of and how can listening skills be improved?

## Listen, listen and...listen again

The phenomenon of 'being in my own world' has meant that I tend to ignore or fail to absorb what others are saying. In addition, my short attention span and poor concentration levels in some situations lead to my missing important information. This has sometimes agitated other people. These factors have impacted upon me in many situations, whether on a one-to-one basis or in group settings.

According to Jane Clarke, everyone finds listening difficult and listening effectively is 'quite difficult to do properly and requires terrific powers of concentration and tenacity to do 100 per cent of the time' (Clarke 1999, p.31). It is, however, the one skill that, perhaps along with understanding and getting along with others, I have worked at hard to get right!

Clarke identifies three different levels of listening:

1.  *Superficial listening.* Here someone will pick up only the thread of what a person is saying. In essence someone has not really heard the other person and the conversation tends to be very much one way. The result is that the person doing the talking tends to lose confidence and interest in what they are trying to say.

    I believe that this has been to a large degree my form of listening and that, from experience, other people can find this highly frustrating.

2.  *Listening for information.* Here all the facts and figures are absorbed but someone is unaware of the feelings and emotions that accompany what an individual is saying. As a result, pleas for help are ignored and symptoms rather than causes are fixed. A person with AS is particularly likely to listen in this way, especially when dealing with staff on a personal basis.

3.  *Listening for feelings and emotions.* Here someone is much more aware of what is going on behind the words. Non-verbal signals are looked for and observed and any questioning is more probing. Questions are more 'why' things happen or 'why' a person has acted this way, and enables the listener to get to the heart of the problem. This also makes the other person feel important and valued as an individual.

There is much that is useful in the above. I try to remain conscious in meetings or when talking to people of the need to concentrate all the time and to really listen. I try to look for messages outside of the stated facts. It is sometimes difficult but I find that, if I make a concerted effort, I can do it and it eradicates many problems and difficulties that would arise later as a result.

Many people with Asperger Syndrome are thought to 'think in pictures' – the title of Temple Grandin's best-selling book that has given some of the best insight into the cognitive processes of people with AS. Grandin states that: 'I do not naturally assimilate information that most people take for granted'. Most people think in a combination of words and vague, generalised pictures.

According to Grandin, people with autism excel at visual spatial skills but have poorer verbal skills. I often find it difficult to communicate a view lucidly in verbal form and find it easier to analyse, process and determine information when it is spatially laid out. By doing this I can 'build up' a picture based around an idea or a problem and add to it. Again, this is similar to Grandin's experience of her thoughts moving from video-like, specific images to generalisations and concepts. Grandin likens it to building a video library.

I have found my experiences in the world of business invaluable. Though my MBA has given me a conceptual framework which I can use as a guide to build strategies and plans, I have been able to use both good and bad experiences in the workplace as 'benchmarks' for future reference. When analogous situations occur later on, I can refer to these previous, practical experiences to ensure that I take the most effective action.

Grandin also talks about observing others, 'photographing' their work and copying their styles. George and Derek have been tremendous mentors for me. Whenever I find myself in a difficult position and searching for a solution I try to imagine how they would act in the same situation. In addition, I practise. My cognitive processes dictate that I need to do this but practice really does instil into me techniques and ensures that they remain firmly entrenched in my behavioural patterns.

There are other traits that are associated with my condition that have impacted upon my general working style and performance. Making improvements to these has also greatly enhanced my management and effectiveness.

One has been my generally lower level of work productivity. Overall, I perceived my work productivity to be lower than that of many of my colleagues or, at least, it takes me longer than others to complete certain tasks.

In general, I find motivation difficult and facing a task hard unless it has a degree of urgency. In many ways this is counterproductive and a source of anxiety and stress later. As previously identified, by putting off a task until the last moment, I am under more pressure when I do come around to dealing with it, thus fueling my anxiety.

Second, I find my concentration on a task variable; my mind not only wanders to other unrelated subjects, but I tend to leave one project and move on to another before returning later to the original task. I find myself easily distracted and diverted to other issues and have a tendency to work at numerous tasks simultaneously in a piecemeal fashion. The net effect is that I 'chip away' at projects and fail to give each my full attention at any one time. This has the further consequence that my mind is not focused on any one project totally and I am less able to recollect facts fully when I return to a subject later.

Related to the last problem is poor time management. I have been guilty of approaching my work schedule in a haphazard fashion, picking up whatever tasks immediately spring to mind, as opposed to identifying my priorities, their requirements and systematically working my way through them.

If a task is difficult or, more pertinently, lacks appeal, I tend to put it to one side until a later, more appropriate moment. The end result is that something that was unappealing but doable then becomes a bigger issue psychologically later.

I have also tended to worry over whether I have done something adequately or perfectly, rather than accepting that there are some tasks that I need to gain experience in and learn as I progress. I have come to learn and accept that I cannot produce perfect results every time!

Now, the first thing I do is slow down. My mind and physiology have a tendency to race and I feel the need to have to do something immediately and quickly. Now, I prepare myself for each day by setting out my stall beforehand, relaxing and getting things around me organised. I have always been an early starter and find that preparing early and getting myself together mentally helps to prepare me for the day and the tasks ahead.

I then think carefully about what I need to do: what I need; who I need to speak to and what the deadlines are. This enables me to then plan my schedule accordingly by making a simple list and working to it.

Importantly, I have to consider how what I am trying to achieve will impact on others. Previously, my insular working method has meant that I have not always accounted for this, with the result that I have failed to forewarn others of my requirements in sufficient time to meet deadlines. I have come to appreciate that it is vital to identify early what is required from people, and give them adequate warning. By thinking ahead in this way, I avoid potential pitfalls and problems appearing later.

The most important thing, along with ensuring that I slow down, is that I make a start. Often this is the most difficult thing to do, but unless I just begin something important immediately, I tend to prevaricate or think of other things that I could do instead.

Usually, in the first few moments of approaching a task, I find it difficult to concentrate and look for reasons to divert my attention elsewhere. By forcing myself to start slowly and gradually ease my way into a task I begin to focus and get into the job in hand and then work productively. Consequently, I insist that I stick to a project and fight through the initial mental barrier that causes me to prevaricate.

If a task is difficult or unattractive, I make myself address that first to avoid allowing it to fester and become an 'issue'. Clearing undesirable tasks is also motivational in so far as it frees my mind and stops me thinking about something that I dislike doing. In addition, I do not defer as this creates pressure.

I have also learnt of the need to pay close attention to detail. I have at times been guilty of not checking the finer points within my work and of producing incomplete or sloppy work. Now I ensure that I check everything carefully before submitting, to avoid careless mistakes; this is especially important if the subject matter is of little interest to me personally. I consider carefully what impression my work will give and what its impact will be on others. I want to ensure that my presentation is of a high standard, so effectively communicating my thoughts and intentions.

Finally, I focus on productivity. I try to make sure that every working moment I am doing something that contributes to my job task. It may be just reading to improve my general subject knowledge, but I do it to ensure that I am working, developing incrementally and delivering each day.

As with all the lessons that I have learnt, and which have been outlined in this book, acquiring the aforementioned skills has contributed greatly towards my work performance. I always pay close attention to these detailed work processes and to what goes on around me. In this way, my productivity and the quality of my output have improved immensely, and my management effectiveness has been significantly enhanced.

## Key development points

- In your work situation, find the right level in terms of your intellectual requirements. Do not underestimate yourself or your abilities, but do not place yourself in a situation that exceeds your cognitive capabilities; this helps avoid unnecessary anxiety.

- Be receptive to, and conscious of, the dynamics operating within groups. Work to become an accepted part of any group and interact with it by contributing and initiating communication with members. Continuously evaluate where you stand within any group and act to bring an end to any negative projections that are directed towards you.

- Reduce pressure by undertaking learning outside of the work environment. Find solutions from other sources and practice them so as to acquire and master skills to resolve shortcomings and prevent future pressure.

- Prepare thoroughly for meetings. Seek to make a positive contribution, identify any potential points of contention and think through carefully beforehand any arguments that you put forward. Ensure that any materials presented are accurate and of a high standard.

- Acknowledge the viewpoints and opinions of others: it may gain you their support. Where you cannot share the viewpoint of another person, be constructive in your challenge, rather than negative or critical.

- Do not necessarily accept at face value what you are told. Question the validity of any statements or proposals, and challenge those that do not seem to you to be correct or accurate.

- Listen effectively. Through practice, acquire the ability to listen carefully and consistently. Register fully what is said, and listen for the emotion behind the verbal message.

- Manage your time carefully and systematically. Think ahead and anticipate hurdles such as time limits, resources and the availability and time of others. By planning ahead, you can avoid the stress that results from being pressed for time.

- Slow down, make a start and ease into work tasks gradually. Persevere with a task until it is completed and do not allow yourself to become distracted by other projects and issues. Clear undesirable tasks, rather than allowing them to linger and 'fester'.

- Do not demand perfection immediately. Strive to produce first-class work but acknowledge that not everything can be done perfectly and completely straight away. View new tasks as a learning process that can be added to and enhanced later.

- Pay attention to, and check, the detail. Go over initial work to identify omissions and erase minor errors, so as to avoid creating any impression of carelessness. Consider the impact on others of your work; in this way you will ensure that you communicate most effectively your thoughts and intentions.

# 14 Reflections

I have found writing this book to be enormously beneficial; by doing so, I have gained an insight and learnt more about myself. The more I learn and discover, the more I understand.

And that is what makes things easier and continues to raise my confidence. I know that tomorrow I will be better equipped than I am today to face any difficulties that emanate from my Asperger Syndrome and this makes it easier for me to move forward. I work consistently at the difficulties that my condition presents on an ongoing basis by the variety of methods that I have found and devised.

To begin with I have become a people watcher. Whereas before I was generally unconcerned and uninterested in the behaviour and actions of others around me, I now watch people assiduously. I watch, take note and analyse how they react and respond in different situations, particularly those in which they come under pressure or are criticised.

In particular, I gauge closely the methods and approach of successful people, the ones who seem to be able to deal effectively with others. George was a great mentor in this area. Never losing his temper, he would always approach problems from a conciliatory perspective and never made an issue personal – an important lesson and one that is high on my mental list of priorities. Today, I steel myself to never look towards someone disparagingly from a personal perspective in a business environment. Over time I have built up a kind of mental library upon which I can draw on how to react in given situations with certain types of people.

I have also made a lot of effort to read and learn more about relationships, emotions and psychology in general. I read books on subjects such as NLP (Neuro-Linguistic Programming), and have also studied Open

University (OU) courses on psychology that have greatly aided my understanding. The OU course on Social Psychology proved to be particularly useful.

I watch visual mediums more closely with a much greater emphasis on understanding interpersonal factors. Before, I was attracted to TV programmes and films that were factually orientated and paid little attention to the personal relationships that were built into the scripts to augment the subject matter. Now, I make a conscious effort to try and follow the development of individual characters within a film or drama documentary and make it a focal point of learning about the emotional factors that impact upon them.

Strange though it is to admit it, I have also become a viewer of soap operas such as *EastEnders*. Though I still find the story lines simplistic and artificial in many ways, the programme does elevate my thinking around relationships and the possible ways to deal with different character types. I have become more able to recognise different, broad characters and the programme has helped to raise the importance of interpersonal relationships on my mental map.

I am also far more conscious of my personal appearance and mannerisms and take more care as to how I present myself. My dress code is more in keeping with my surroundings and I recognise the importance of sensitivity to detail in this area.

Whilst in meetings and elsewhere, I try to ensure that I retain my space and do not encroach on that of others. I am also more careful with small talk and appreciate to a greater degree that there is a time and a place for it and that there are other occasions when not to indulge.

Of great assistance with this process of self-awareness has been listening to and viewing myself. During my time with the leisure company I was required to undertake an interview that later appeared on national television. When I watched a tape recording of the interview later, I was struck at how tense, rigid and nervous I appeared. Whilst accepting that I was likely to be all of these things to some degree whilst being filmed, it was far more pronounced than I anticipated.

The experience enabled me to identify where I needed to make changes and this has helped me to present myself more professionally subsequently. Specifically I slow down when I speak, make more pronounced hand movements and increase the level of facial interaction.

In terms of how I sound, I was struck by a telephone discussion that was played back to me at a later date following a work conversation with a journalist. My voice was somewhat monotonous, lacked emotion and was delivered in one, unvarying pitch. Today I try to modulate my speech and sound more upbeat when I speak to others, particularly at the beginning and end of conversations.

Ultimately, however, I believe that being myself is the most important thing of all. Though I am different, I have come to appreciate that I face many of the same challenges in the professional workplace as others. By understanding my personal characteristics, how they impact upon others and by proactively working to reduce their negative effects, I know that I can succeed in responsible, senior management positions.

Moreover, Asperger Syndrome has given me skills that others do not possess and that are immensely valuable and important in a management capacity. The ability to analyse deeply and see the wider picture are unique talents than confer upon me a real advantage.

In short, I do not view my condition as a disadvantage. By utilising the advantages that it proffers whilst learning to overcome some of its other effects, I have become a competent, effective and increasingly successful manager. My progress and achievements are testimony to that.

# References

Attwood, T. (1998) *Asperger's Syndrome: A Guide for Parents and Professionals.* London: Jessica Kingsley Publishers.

Clarke, J. (1999) *Office Politics: A Survival Guide.* London: The Industrial Society.

Datlow Smith, M., Belcher, R.G. and Juhrs, P.D. (1995) *A Guide to Successful Employment for Individuals with Autism.* Baltimore, MD: Paul H. Brookes Publishing Co.

Grandin, T. (1996) *Thinking In Pictures.* New York: Vintage Books.

Matthews, A. (1990) *Making Friends: A Guide to Getting Along with People.* Singapore: Media Masters.

Morgan, H. and Thomas, K. (1996) 'Group Processes: A Psychodynamic Perspective.' In M. Wetherell (ed.) *Identities, Groups and Social Issues.* Thousand Oaks, CA: Sage Publications.

Wetherell, M. (ed.) (1996) *Identities, Groups and Social Issues.* Thousand Oaks, CA: Sage Publications.

# Index